Twayne's United States Authors Series

Edgar Allan Poe

TUSAS 4
(Second Edition)

Edgar Allan Poe

EDGAR ALLAN POE

By VINCENT BURANELLI

SECOND EDITION

TWAYNE PUBLISHERS
A DIVISION OF G. K. HALL & CO., BOSTON

Library of Congress Cataloging in Publication Data

Buranelli, Vincent.
Edgar Allan Poe.

(Twayne's United States author series; TUSAS 4)
Bibliography: p. 148-59.
Includes index.
1. Poe, Edgar Allan, 1809 - 1849—Criticism and interpretation.
PS2638.B87 1977 818'.3'09 77-7265
ISBN 0-8057-7189-1

MANUFACTURED IN THE UNITED STATES OF AMERICA

To My Mother

Contents

About the Author

Vincent Buranelli is a freelance writer who was born in New York and raised in New Jersey. After serving in the United States Army in the Pacific during World War II, he attended St. John's of Annapolis for the Greek year of the Great Books curriculum. He received his bachelor's degree in philosophy (1947) and his master's degree in political science (1948) at the National University of Ireland, where he learned from Francis Hackett and Constantine Curran, old friends of James Joyce, much of the information he later put into his writing on Joyce. From Dublin, he went to Cambridge University where he took his doctorate in history (1951) under the supervision of Michael Oakeshott and J.P.T. Bury. While at Cambridge, he wrote and lectured on the history of ideas in France; and Oakeshott, then editor of the *Cambridge Journal,* published his first article, a study of Pascal's political theory. F.R. Leavis, a Fellow of his College (Downing), introduced him to the type of literary criticism represented by *Scrutiny,* which Leavis was editing. Dr. Buranelli attended Bertrand Russell's famous "at homes" at Trinity College, and later wrote his impressions of Russell for *Prairie Schooner* (1955) and the *Journal of the Bertrand Russell Archives* (1975).

Before returning home, he married Non Gillespie of Glasgow, who is a writer and linguist. After returning home, he became an associate of Lowell Thomas, a Kaltenborn Fellow in Journalism, a staff writer for American Heritage, and a senior editor for Silver Burdett. He has contributed to many publications, including *Proceedings of the American Philosophical Society, McGraw-Hill Encyclopedia of World Drama, William and Mary Quarterly,* and *New-York Historical Society Quarterly.* He has published two volumes in Twayne's United States Authors Series —*Edgar Allan Poe* (1961) and *Josiah Royce* (1964). He has published one volume in Twayne's Rulers and Statesmen of the World Series—*Louis XIV* (1966). His other books are: *The Trial of Peter Zenger* (1957), *The King and the Quaker: a Study of William Penn and James II* (1962), and *The Wizard from Vienna: Franz Anton Mesmer* (1975). Forthcoming is *The Nile,* coauthored by Nan Buranelli.

He also appears on the platform and on radio with a lecture entitled "Doctor Mesmer," based on his book *The Wizard from Vienna,* one chapter of which—"A Note on Poe and Mesmerism"—he adapted for use in this second edition of *Edgar Allan Poe.*

Preface, Second Edition

The late Thomas O. Mabbott used to say: "Books on Poe always sell." As usual where Poe was concerned, Mabbott was right. Since interest in Poe never wanes, even an unpretentious contribution to the subject may achieve some success, and to this fact I attribute the call for a second edition of this volume fifteen years after the appearance of the first edition.

Any author revising his earlier work is faced with an invitation and a challenge to reflect about its contents. He will, on a close rereading, inevitably discover things that might have been done differently then and ought to be done differently now—from factual mistakes or infelicitous prose to important topics inadequately treated. Moreover, time has changed both the author and his subject. His judgments, affected by his increased experience, cannot be identical in all respects with those he once held; nor can he think about his subject except as it has been altered by recent scholarship. Such changes in the author and the subject dictate at least in part the character of the second edition.

Most of the first edition, nevertheless, should withstand scrutiny unless new evidence compels a drastic shift of opinion as in the discovery of the Boswell and Lafayette papers. Nothing that revolutionary has occurred in Poe studies. This second edition therefore retains much of the first edition although the corrections, revisions, and additions are substantial.

Perhaps the most important point about Poe scholarship during the past fifteen years is that it lost its most distinguished and devoted practitioner when Mabbott died. He was a friend and mentor to many of us in the field, and he not only criticized my manuscript chapter by chapter but also gave me the benefit of the erudition he was putting into his *Collected Works of Edgar Allan Poe* for the Harvard University Press. The tribute to him in my original preface was not mere courtesy or an attempt to attach a respected name to my book. It was a statement of fact.

Mabbott had a balanced view of Poe at a time when unbalanced views were not uncommon. Biographers were picturing Poe as a drunkard, a drug fiend, a necrophilist, and an obsessed mind little short of insanity. Critics were saying that Poe's vulgarities and abnormalities corrupted his writings. Mabbott put forward the simple proposition that no enduring artist could have been like that, and he proved his point in the notes, articles, introductions, and private conversations for which he was so famous. If any one man set the trend of Poe studies into the present, Mabbott did.

This is not to say, which would be absurd, that Poe scholarship was ever a one-man show. Mabbott's older contemporary, Killis Campbell, preceded him in approaching Poe realistically, rationally, and without preconceptions. Major figures who made their reputations at about the same time as Mabbott included Arthur Hobson Quinn (on Poe's biography), John Ward Ostrom (on his letters), and Floyd Stovall (on his poetry). Together they cleared away much of the underbrush surrounding Poe. They made it possible for their followers to see through the gossip, malice, and mythology that dated from the time when Rufus Wilmot Griswold (Poe's literary executor!) created the horrific Poe in an infamous obituary.

There has been a continuity of scholarship since the age of the giants in that no major school of thought on Poe has vanished. It is easier today to write of him as a sane creative genius, more difficult to write of him as a character from his Gothic tales; but this shift of emphasis does not mean that the former opinion will, or can, oust the latter. Critics are still writing on both sides.

Since less disagreement exists about the facts in the Poe case, criticism to the extent that it is based on facts is more unified than it was. Pure criticism is where most of the disagreements lie, quite naturally because values are the issue, and values escape the empirical test. That Poe was not a drug fiend is established, but that he was a major poet will never be established for those who do not feel it in the reading. Still, the trend in pure criticism is to upgrade Poe. This volume has benefitted from the trend. It is gratifying to note that the final sentence of the text is no longer a subject for derision.

To be specific about this second edition: The structure of the book remains the same even to a repetition of the chapter headings. The content remains that of a critical study in which biography is used to explain the author's works; in other words, the life of Poe is referred to insofar as it throws light on his writings. Chapter 1 has not been altered because it formulates the problem that is the subject of the book, and the terms of the problem have not changed. Chapter 2 has been expanded to include a passage on Mesmerism, an addition necessitated by a simple accumulation of knowledge by the author.

Chapter 3 has some additional pages about the distinction between Poe the man and Poe the artist. Since this distinction is fundamental to my whole interpretation of Poe, I felt that something more was demanded than the rather cursory treatment in the first edition. One way to make the distinction clear is to explain why the periodic disorientation of Poe's faculties did not vitiate his Gothic tales. I have tried to do this by showing that there is a fallacy in the argument from faculty psychology.

Chapter 4 contains the most important revision in the book. Anyone looking back over many years will tend to quarrel with some of his past judgments, and the denial of morality in Poe's short stories gave me more trouble than any other passage in the first edition. I did not and do not attribute to Poe the attitude of Walter Pater (the pursuit of beauty is essential morality), much less that of Oscar Wilde (art has nothing to do with morality). To say, however, that "Poe does not touch morality" is too strong if not misleading, and what followed in this passage now seems to me to have been ineptly stated. The passage has been rewritten although the substance of the argument is the same. An added page on the detective story is much less significant; it is there to place Poe more clearly within one tradition he created.

Chapter 5 has a new sub-chapter on the condemnation of Poe's poetry as incurably vulgar. This is another contention that seems to me mistaken, based as it is on a misconception of how meter is related to meaning in poetry. I committed an oversight in failing to deal with it forthrightly in my first treatment of Poe's verse. Chapter 6 was too lenient to Poe as a critic, so a page has been added to show where his bias lay. Chapter 7 had to be rewritten and expanded because it concerns Poe's achievement and influence, and therefore had to be brought up to date in the light of recent scholarship and criticism.

The bibliography has been recast and enlarged. In my original preface, I mentioned the enormous number of writings about Poe, an embarrassment of riches that has become much more embarrassing since then. Fortunately, full bibliographies now exist, something that rendered unnecessary any attempt at a comprehensive listing of publications covering fifteen years. The footnotes have naturally been changed to parallel changes in the text.

Some blemishes in the first edition have been removed. Among other misdemeanors, I misspelled the first name of Erle Stanley Gardner, and suffered the mortification of being silently corrected by four translators.

On one particular approach to Poe, this edition stands four-square where the last one stood. As I grow older, I become increasingly less impressed or amused by the vagaries of psychoanalytical criticism. Of course it is legitimate for a critic to make use of such tools as Freud's theory of dreams, the archetypes of Jung, and the analysis of personality from Horney to Fromm. What is illegitimate is the absurd and gratuitous symbolism to which the more bizarre psychoanalysts resort. It is difficult not to feel impatient with Marie Bonaparte when she informs us that fear of castration is the main theme of "The Black Cat."

The interpretation of Poe in this book remains eclectic. I have learned from scholars who belong to different schools of thought, and I am willing to see, for example, that Poe is in his Gothic stories by turns a realist, an ironist, a satirist, a hoaxer, or an actor. No single explanation will do, in my opinion, because Poe made his decision each time with an eye on the literary market place.

There are no startling novelties or recantations in this second edition. The verdict remains the same. For me, Poe is neither a cousin, nor an adolescent, nor a provincial, but a great writer whom I read with continual pleasure.

VINCENT BURANELLI

Lawrenceville,
New Jersey

Preface, First Edition

So much scholarship has been devoted to Poe in recent years, so many explanatory books and articles written, that this seems an appropriate moment for a new evaluation of him as thinker and writer.

This study is primarily critical. It assimliates the latest research, adopting facts and judgment offered by many experts working in the field; but it does so selectively and according to a definite interpretation that emerges from an examination of Poc's works. Every viable interpretation of Poe must have this character of independent thought since the secondary authorites are so divided about his worth, and this volume stands or falls with the validity of its guiding principles.

Although the limits prescribed forbid any exhaustive treatment of the subject, the scope is wide enough to cover the major aspects of Poe's achievement and influence, and of his life insofar as it relates to them. This study is, therefore, complete in the sense that nothing of the first importance had to be passed over for want of space. It is complete as far as it goes, and it goes far enough to let the reader judge for himself whether or not the analysis is justified by the facts.

The author is grateful to Porfessor Thomas O. Mabbott for a critical reading of the manuscript. Professor Mabbott, whose forthcoming complete edition of Poe for the Harvard University Press will the definitive one, gave generously of his time and his knowledge; and, although he cannot be held responsible for the result, he contributed much to making this book less defective than it would otherwise have been.

V. B.

Penn's Neck
Princeton, New Jersey

Chronology

1809 Edgar Poe is born in Boston, January 19.
1811 His mother dies in Richmond; and, now orphaned, he is taken in by the John Allans and christened Edgar Allan Poe.
1815 He goes to England with the Allans.
1820 He returns to Richmond with the Allans.
1826 He enters the University of Virginia and becomes engaged to Elmira Royster, only to have the engagement interrupted by her parents.
1827 He leaves the university, quarrels with John Allan, goes to Boston, enlists in the U.S. Army. Publications: *Tamerlane and Other Poems.*
1829 He is discharged from the army following the death of Mrs. Allan. Publications: *Al Aaraaf, Tamerlane and Minor Poems.*
1830 He enters West Point but deliberately gets himself expelled for want of financial support by John Allan.
1831 He begins a period of obscurity in New York and Baltimore. Publications: *Poems.*
1832 His whereabouts remain uncertain. Publications: "Metzengerstein."
1833 He wins a prize from the Baltimore *Saturday Visiter* for "MS. Found in a Bottle."
1834 John Allan dies without mentioning Poe in his will.
1835 Poe becomes editor of the *Southern Literary Messenger* in December. Publications: "Berenice," "Morella," "Hans Pfaal."
1836 He marries his cousin, Virginia Clemm. Publications: the review of Drake's *Culprit Fay.*
1837 Forced to leave the *Southern Literary Messenger* in January, he goes to New York.
1838 He publishes "Arthur Gordon Pym" before leaving for Philadelphia where "Ligeia" appears.
1839 He becomes an editor of *Burton's Gentleman's Magazine* in June. Publications: "William Wilson," "The Fall of the House of Usher," "The Conversation of Eiros and Charmion," "The Haunted Palace."

1840 He works with cryptograms, then leaves *Burton's Gentleman's Magazine* in June with plans for his own periodical to be called the *Penn Magazine.* Publications: *Tales of the Grotesque and Arabesque,* "The Man of the Crowd," the review of Longfellow's *Voices of the Night.*

1841 He becomes an editor of *Graham's Magazine* in April. Publications: "The Murders in the Rue Morgue," "A Descent into the Maelstrom," the review of Macaulay's *Essays.*

1842 He leaves *Graham's Magazine* in May, still hoping for his own journal, now to be called the *Stylus.* Publications: "Eleanora," "The Oval Portrait," "The Masque of the Red Death," "The Mystery of Marie Roget," the reviews of Dickens' *Barnaby Rudge,* Longfellow's *Ballads and Other Poems,* Hawthorne's *Twice-Told Tales.*

1843 He wins a prize from the Philadelphia *Dollar Newspaper* for "The Gold Bug." Publications: "The Pit and the Pendulum," "The Tell-Tale Heart," "The Black Cat."

1844 He moves to New York, his home for the rest of his life. Publications: "The Balloon Hoax," "The Premature Burial," "The Oblong Box."

1845 He publishes "The Raven," which causes an overnight sensation, and becomes an editor of the *Broadway Journal* in March. Publications: *Tales, The Raven and Other Poems.*

1846 After presiding over the end of the *Broadway Journal* in January, he moves to the cottage at Fordham. Publications: "The Cask of Amontillado," "The Literati," "The Philosphy of Composition," the review of Bryant's *Poems.*

1847 After a harrowing illness, Virginia Poe dies on January 29 leaving Poe despondent. Publications: "The Domain of Arnheim," "Ulalume."

1848 Poe has his romance with Mrs. Whitman, and delivers "The Poetic Principle" as a lecture. Publications: "Eureka."

1849 Poe has his romances with Mrs. Richmond and Mrs. Shelton (Elmira Royster). Publications: "For Annie," "Annabel Lee," "Eldorado," "The Bells," the review of Lowell's *Fable for Critics.*
Poe dies in Baltimore, October 7.

CHAPTER 1

The Problem of Poe

EDGAR Allan Poe is the most complex personality in the entire gallery of American authors. No one else fuses, as he does, such discordant psychological attributes, or offers to the world an appearance so various. No one else stands at the center of a mystery so profound. Hawthorne, Melville and Faulkner are, by comparison with Poe, easy enough to classify, while Edwards, Cooper and Hemingway emerge with crystal clarity. Poe resists easy interpretation and broad generalization. Any plausible analysis of his work, like any authentic story of his life, must begin with this primary and essential truth.

The problem of Poe concerns much more than the dark side of his genius. Yet it cannot be denied that he himself has obscured the dimensions of the problem by the very success with which he writes of horror, terror, strange fantasies and psychological abnormalities. He has, by the very effectiveness of his Gothic imaginings, encouraged the criticism that concentrates on his pyrotechnics to the exclusion of almost everything else. He has helped to sketch the popular image that derives from such works as "The Raven," "The Murders in the Rue Morgue," "The Fall of the House of Usher," "The Pit and the Pendulum," "The Tell-Tale Heart," and "The Black Cat."

When these titles monopolize the attention, it is only natural that the central body of Poe's work should seem to be a tissue of nightmares—a literary fabric shot with disease, madness, death, hideous murders, ghastly exhumations, shrieks in the night. It is only natural that the sanity of the author should become suspect, and that he should appear to be a gifted psychopath describing with consummate artistry his personal instabilities and abnormalities. Hence the idea—old, persistent and widespread—that the somber figure of Edgar Allan Poe stalks forever through the pages of his stories and poems. He is declared to have only one endlessly repeated male character—himself. He is pictured as appearing and reappearing under the guises of his melancholic, neurasthenic, hallucinated, mad and half-mad protagonists: Roderick Usher, Egaeus, William Wilson, Cornelius Wyatt, Montresor, Hop-Frog, Metzengerstein.

This conception of Poe is not merely popular in the sense that it appeals to the reading public at large. It has been alive among literary critics ever since Walt Whitman gave it his support in a passage that never ceases to be quoted:

> In a dream I once had, I saw a vessel on the sea, at midnight, in a storm. It was no great full-rigg'd ship, nor majestic steamer, steering firmly through the gale, but seem'd one of those superb little schooner yachts I had often seen lying anchor'd, rocking so jauntily, in the waters around New York, or up Long Island sound—now flying uncontroll'd with torn sails and broken spars through the wild sleet and the winds and waves of the night. On the deck was a slender, slight, beautiful figure, a dim man, apparently enjoying the terror, the murk, and the dislocation of which he was the centre and the victim. That figure of my lurid dream might stand for Edgar Poe, his spirit, his fortunes, and his poems—themselves all lurid dreams.[1]

Although Whitman's judgment cannot be pronounced dead, the function of a large part of Poe criticism has been to dissolve his "lurid dream," diluting it with facts he did not consider, weakening its internal coherence, and causing it to disintegrate. Judgments contrary to his have been put forward. Poe has been called an actor and a humorist.[2] He has been described as an artist pure and simple who deliberately chose his themes for effect and constructed his art with building-blocks no more substantial than those provided by his creative imagination, so that to consider him obsessed because the narrator of "The Black Cat" is obsessed is like assuming that Cooper was an Indian or Irving a Dutch colonial.[3]

If Poe's normal traits are being stressed too much today, it is an error on the right side, one that should enable us to strike a balance closer to the truth than either of the extremes. That he can ever be categorized neatly either biographically or artistically is not to be expected, for there is too much room for doubt and disputation when the ideas, moods and temperament of so difficult a personality are under investigation. But at least we are aware of the multifarious elements in him and his literature.

Poe is both a dreamy fantasist ("The Valley of Unrest") and a cerebral logician ("The Purloined Letter"). He lingers with science ("Eureka") and is chilled by its abstractions ("To Science"). He resolutely closes his eyes to factual reality ("Ligeia") and examines it in detail ("Landor's Cottage"). He works with melancholy ("The Fall of the House of Usher"), and with humor ("Why the Little Frenchman Wears His Hand in a Sling"); with burlesque ("Bon Bon"), and with realism ("The Cask of Amontillado"). He probes fascinated, into horrible obsessions ("The Tell-Tale Heart"), and gazes, enchanted, at ethereal beauty ("To Helen").

It is false to call him little more than an artist of nightmares, hallucinations, insane crimes and weird beauties, little more than an intuitive poetic genius dabbling in pretentious logic when he is not lost in the black forest of pathological psychology. Nor is he a frigid allegorist living in an ivory tower safely away from the contamination of the world. Poe is a dreamer (in the widest sense of the term), and that is where an analytical study may properly begin; but it must not end until it has accounted for Poe the rationalist, the scientist, the hoaxer, the humorist, and the literary and social critic.

CHAPTER 2

Retreat from Reality

POE was the type who has to escape from the vulgarities of practical life on occasion or else go mad. Like many another artist, he turned to his imagination for something better than a world of office politics, boarding-house landladies, social snubs, hounding debts, and the cash nexus. His imagination took some peculiar twists, not always at his bidding, but at least it provided him with materials that he could work up into literature.

I *Romanticism*

The danger of inferring directly from Poe's morbid subjects to his life and mind becomes clearer when he is set within his historical era, and within a continuing literary tradition. He was not the first to unite the beautiful and the strange in poetry, nor did he originate the idea of putting fantasy, horror and terror into short stories. He came upon these practices when they were already a standard part of European literature and had made a strong appearance in American literature. That is, he stepped into the swirling current of the romantic movement.

Poe started out as a romantic of a type familiar to his time, America's closest analogue of Byron, Keats, Shelley, Hugo, Heine, Leopardi, Pushkin. If he never conformed precisely to the type, if as time passed he marred his romanticism and corrupted it with extraneous and incompatible qualities, its presence can be identified in him throughout his career from "Tamerlane" (1827) and "Al Aaraaf" (1829) to "Eureka" (1848) and "For Annie" (1849).

He first came before the reading public wearing the mantle of the romantic poet, striking the Byronic notes of pride, power, pessimism, love, bereavement and death in *Tamerlane and Other Poems*. The romantic poets tended to mature precociously, and Poe published this volume when he was only eighteen. *They* felt, almost to a man, that they were cut off from most of humanity by their genius; *he* felt exactly the same about himself. He formulated the thought in a passage of "Marginalia" that, despite its apparent impersonality, can only apply to himself.

> I have sometimes amused myself by endeavoring to fancy what would be the fate of any individual gifted, or rather accursed, with an intellect *very* far superior to that of his race. Of course, he would be conscious of his superiority; nor could he (if otherwise constituted as man is) help manifesting his consciousness. Thus he would make himself enemies at all points. And since his opinions and speculations would widely differ from those of *all* mankind—that he would be considered a madman, is evident. How horribly painful such a condition! Hell could invent no greater torture than that of being charged with abnormal weakness on account of being abnormally strong.[1]

Romanticism implied resistance to authority since the romantic at his most characteristic would not concede the superiority of anyone or anything to himself. Poe did not concede it either, although he never was committed so far in practical affairs as to become a rebel like Byron. In "Eureka" Poe asserts: "No thinking being lives who, at some luminous point of his life of thought, has not felt himself lost amid the surges of futile efforts at understanding, or believing, that anything exists *greater than his own soul.*"[2] What Poe meant was that he himself had experienced this frustration. No more genuinely romantic notion has ever been expressed in American literature.

Romanticism was partly a pose with its devotees. Poe, more fortunate than most, had a number of poses available for use depending on the situation. When he wanted to play the Byronic aristocrat, he could point to his family history, going back beyond the ambitions, frailties and failures of his parents to a somewhat mythical ancestry of Norman, German, British and Irish bloodlines, and to a more substantial paternal grandfather who had acted as quartermaster for the patriot armies during the Revolution and been an acquaintance of Lafayette. It was possible for Poe to see more than a touch of aristocracy in this inheritance—one he felt he lived up to just by being a gentleman of the Old Dominion. "I am," he liked to say, "a Virginian."

Alternatively, and also in good romantic fashion, he could appear as the tragic hero—the misbegotten offspring of strolling players. He enjoyed the absurd rumor that he was the grandson of Benedict Arnold. He had a penchant for being mysterious about himself, and at various periods of his life he went by pseudonyms like Henri le Rannet and Edgar A. Perry.

True to his romanticism, Poe invented a Byronic expedition to Europe in the name of heroism and freedom. He tells us that he set out to help the Greeks win their fight for liberty, failed to reach Greece, was somehow detoured into Russia, and only managed to return home through the good offices of the American consul in Saint Petersburg. It was the kind of jaunt he would like to have made—in retrospect.[3]

He adopted the *poetic* pose of the romantics as a matter of course, and this was something he could do the more plausibly since he looked like a poet. He painted a self-portrait in his description of Roderick Usher: "cadaverousness of complexion; an eye large, liquid, and luminous beyond comparison; lips somewhat thin and very pallid . . . a nose of delicate Hebrew model . . . a finely moulded chin . . . hair of more than web-like softness and tenuity . . . altogether a countenance not easily to be forgotten." This description can, or must, be read into various other of Poe's fictional characters. He evidently thought it fitted himself, and his portraits indicate that it did. His looking like a poet never damaged the effect when he declaimed his verse in drawingrooms.

Poe had the flair for dramatics that a romantic poet ought to have. His parents left him a theatrical heritage on which to build, and although he did not imitate them by becoming an actor, although he lacked the ability to write for the theatre and never finished his single play ("Politian"), his works abound in stage settings and melodramatic effects. These are evident in the garish lighting of "The Masque of the Red Death," the deliberately darkened rooms of "The Purloined Letter," the fantastic architecture of "The Domain of Arnheim," the baroque furnishings complemented by incense and soft music of "The Assignation," and the wild masquerade of "Hop-Frog."

The early nineteenth century was an era when pseudo-Orientalism was in fashion. Poets went to the East—or to what they considered to be the East—for names resonant with mysterious, romantic syllables evocative of distant lands, remote times, and strange peoples. Coleridge's "Kubla Khan," Byron's "The Giaour" and Moore's "Lalla Rookh" remain as permanent examples of the type. So do Poe's "Israfel" and "Al Aaraaf."

It was an era of voyages to the ends of the earth (Poe's "Arthur Gordon Pym") and of journeys into the wilderness (Poe's "Astoria" and "The Journal of Julius Rodman").

The early nineteenth century was beguiled by things Gothic—quaint folklore, macabre legends, preternatural events, medieval history, forgotten tombs, ruined abbeys. Around these interests grew a whole body of literature profoundly influential on both sides of the Atlantic. From Germany a special brand of lurid Gothicism penetrated into other lands through the startling works of Ludwig Tieck and E. T. A. Hoffmann, author of the popular *Tales Of Hoffmann.* Tieck and Hoffmann gained an international following and were paid everywhere the compliment of imitation. Their potent art crossed the ocean, and in America it affected the fiction of Charles Brockden Brown and Nathaniel Hawthorne.[4]

The Gothic element provided Poe with a literary milieu perfectly adapted to his taste and talent. He may never have read Tieck and Hoffmann in the original, but he was fully aware of their contribution from translations and from their British, French, and American followers. The question of "Germanic gloom" as a proper vehicle for fiction formed the subject of a long discussion in *Blackwood's Magazine,* a periodical Poe followed closely. The importance of *Blackwood's* in his artistic development can scarcely be overestimated, for it provided him with the theory of the Gothic tale and with practical examples of how to write one; and at the same time it revealed to him that valuable source material could be extracted from case histories in the annals of crime and psychiatry.[5]

As an editor, Poe kept abreast of the current literary trends; as critic and writer, he handled the Gothic theme with a perspicacious insight into its value for literary purposes—for *his* purposes. He recognized the imprint of Tieck's hand on Hawthorne's *Twice-Told Tales;* he makes Baron Von Jung of "Mystification" a relative of Tieck; he informs his readers that a volume of Tieck lay on the table in Roderick Usher's study. Poe's horror stories were not, therefore, written in a haphazard way, but rather conformed to his theory of what he was trying to do. He set forth his theory in a letter to Thomas White, for whom he worked on the *Southern Literary Messenger.*

The history of all Magazines shows plainly that those which have attained celebrity were indebted for it to articles *similar in nature to Berenice*

. . . I say similar in *nature.* You ask me in what does this nature consist? In the ludicrous heightened into the grotesque: the fearful coloured into the horrible: the witty exaggerated into the burlesque: the singular wrought out into the strange and mystical. . . . To be appreciated you must be *read,* and these are invariably sought after with avidity. . . . Such articles are the "M.S. found in a Madhouse" and the "Monos and Daimonos" of the London New Monthly—the "Confessions of an Opium-Eater" and the "Man in a Bell" of Blackwood.[6]

Because his plots so often resemble those he mentions in this statement, Poe was accused by his detractors of being just an echo of the Gothic writers before him. His answer was twofold. In his preface to *Tales of the Grotesque and Arabesque* he confessed to working in a vein already tapped by the Germans and by their European and American imitators. Then, to block the charge of unoriginality and plagiarism, he added emphatically: "If in many of my productions terror has been the thesis, I maintain that terror is not of Germany, but of the soul—that I deduced this terror only from its legitimate sources, and have urged it only to its legitimate results."[7] What Poe is saying is that he added something fundamental to his borrowings by giving old themes an urgency they could not have had on merely literary grounds—an urgency derived, as we shall see, from his personal history. But the existence and popularity of the genre, and Poe's overt and experessed understanding of its pragmatic utility, should be kept in mind when his choice of subjects is under investigation. Poe did not popularize the horrible and the terrible. He specialized in horror and terror because he discovered they were popular.

It was not just a matter of the written word. America, New York in particular, was going through a boom in occultism. Spiritualism flourished along with palm reading, oneiromancy, and magic generally. Ghostly visitations and cosmic revelations came to psychic visionaries. Circles met for seances and listened to table-rapping. Mediums, mystics, sibyls, seers, and prophetesses battened on credulity, always their victims' and occasionally their own.

As today, the line between science and pseudo-science could not be drawn with exactitude. Astronomy had emerged from astrology, and chemistry from alchemy; but what was to be made of phrenology? Franz Joseph Gall spoke as a trained, experienced medical man when he declared the surface of the skull, the famous "bumps," to be an indicator of psychological characteristics located in the brain. There was nothing absurd in his theory until it failed to pass the experimental test.

What was to be made of Mesmerism? This question touches Poe directly because he used Mesmerism in three of his stories—"A Tale of the Ragged Mountains," "Mesmeric Revelation," and "The Facts in the Case of M. Valdemar." The problem presented by Franz Anton Mesmer, who died in 1815 within Poe's lifetime, was that he had the right facts (the trance and the curious phenomena resulting from it) but the wrong theory. Mesmer believed that he put his subjects into his celebrated trance by infusing their nervous systems with "animal magnetism," rays of a universal cosmic fluid. This original theory of the founder lingered after the true theory had been put forward by his followers, namely, that the trance resulted from suggestion in the subject's mind, its cause being psychological rather than physical. When this fact was established, Mesmerism became scientific hypnotism.

Mesmerism had an enormous impact on literature in Europe and America. Poe took his version largely from Chauncey Hare Townshend's *Facts in Mesmerism,* which informed him that one human being could control animal magnetism, channel it through space into the nervous system of another human being, and thereby dominate his ideas, volitions, and emotions. Poe, who believed Townshend's theory, found it an admirable starting-point for a special type of Gothic fiction. In "A Tale of the Ragged Mountains," thought transference from Templeton causes Bedloe to have hallucinations. In "Mesmeric Revelation," Vankirk has preternatural visions while in a trance. In "The Facts in the Case of M. Valdemar," a dying man is mesmerized, and his condition is arrested until the typically Poesque ending:

> As I rapidly made the mesmeric passes, amid ejaculations of "dead! dead!" absolutely *bursting* from the tongue and not from the lips of the sufferer, his whole frame at once—within the space of a single minute, or even less, shrunk—crumbled—absolutely *rotted* away beneath my hands. Upon the bed, before that whole company, there lay a nearly liquid mass of loathsome—of detestable putridity.

Poe ended this story so realistically that more than one reader accepted the ending as factual, something that amused the author because he had achieved a successful hoax in spite of himself.[8]

The elements of the strange, the abnormal, and the weird that Poe singled out for his own purposes, he assimilated into his experience of age-old, hoary, legendary, half-forgotten European antiquities. As a child, he had spent some years in England where he had attended a school at Stoke Newington and had seen the building that sets the stage for "William Wilson" as the story begins: "My earliest recollections of a school-life, are connected with a large, rambling, Elizabethan house, in a misty-looking village of England, where were a vast number of gigantic and gnarled trees, and where all the houses were excessively ancient." Poe often drew upon his memory for his settings, as in "The Fall of the House of Usher," which concerns the fate of a decayed aristocratic family and its moldering Gothic mansion ("House" in both sense of the word). He knew the feeling that comes over an imaginative human being when he meets face-to-face the Gothic past.

The romantic movement was a reaction against classicism and its emphasis on the Olympian wisdom of the abstract intellect. The romantics preferred to be concrete and personal. They abandoned the correct rules of the past; put their faith in individualized experience, asking only that it be imaginative and artistically usable; and sought for new forms in which to express it. Endeavoring to capture values and verities that escaped the intellect, they were willing to consult everything the imagination offered—whether vision or nightmare.[9]

In this willingness, too, Poe was a true romantic. One of his fundamental convictions concerned a peculiar and indubitable knowledge attainable only in dreams. He was not referring to sleep. He meant those wakeful moments which approximate dreams because the individual drifts off into a private world of his own making where the senses cease to bear on mundane reality and the reason ceases to criticize. It is the world of reveries, daydreams, trances, hypnotic states, even attacks of drunkenness and hallucination. The narrator of "Eleanora" speaks for Poe in suggesting that profound truths can be discovered through "disease of thought" and in adding: "They who dream by day are cognizant of many things that escape those who dream only by night. In their grey visions they obtain glimpses of eternity, and thrill, in awaking, to find that they have been upon the verge of the great secret."

Poe appraised these dreams without sleep very highly. Approaching them with a curiosity compounded of poetry and science, he was determined to wrest their secrets from them. He took to inspecting with meticulous exactitude his psychological states when he hovered between sleep and wakefulness, found his mind occupied with shadows of ideas "rather psychical than intellectual," and learned to some degree to control them. He discusses his method in "Marginalia."

These "fancies" have in them a pleasurable ecstasy as far beyond the most pleasurable of the world of wakefulness, or of dreams, as the Heaven of the Northman theology is beyond its Hell. I regard the visions, even as they arise, with an awe which, in some measure, moderates or tranquilizes the ecstasy—I so regard them through a conviction (which seems a portion of the ecstasy itself) that this ecstasy, in itself, is of a character supernal to the Human Nature—is a glimpse of the spirit's outer world. . . . It is as if the five senses were supplanted by five myriad others alien to mortality. . . . In experiments with this end in view, I have proceeded so far as, first, to control (when the bodily and mental health are good) the existence of the condition. . . . I have proceeded so far, secondly, as to prevent the lapse from *the point* of which I speak—the point of blending between wakefulness and sleep—as to prevent at will, I say, the lapse from this border-ground into the dominion of sleep. Not that I can *continue* the condition—not that I can render the point more than a point—but that I can startle myself from the point into wakefulness—*and thus transfer the point itself into the realm of Memory*—convey its impressions, or more properly their recollections, to a situation where (although still for a very brief period) I can survey them with the eye of analysis.[10]

From his subconscious Poe evoked half-dreams of a unique significance. They opened to him a sublime universe past whose borders his faculties could not go in their ordinary wide-awake operations. Not all of his creative insights came to him in this way, but it is to his experiences as a sleep-waker that we owe his vision of ethereal beauty—the vision that produced such poems as "The Sleeper," "Israfel" and "Lenore."

When Poe reviewed *Undine,* he deplored "our anti-romantic national character."[11] That self-defense lurks in the phrase scarcely needs to be said, but the truth in the indictment is not easy to estimate since the American public was romantic in its taste to this extent at least, that it read Gothic stories. It read

Poe's. Cold to most lyric poetry, it appreciated the strange music of "The Raven" and made the poet famous.

Poe could not seriously contend that he was ignored. He *was* misunderstood—not because of his romanticism, but because he left romanticism behind in some of his pioneering expeditions into an artistic universe he discovered. He broke through the conventions handed on to him and became a precursor of symbolism and surrealism by finding new ways to reveal things lying too deep in his psyche to be captured in ordinary word patterns. He experimented with his senses, and noted: "We can at any time double the beauty of an actual landscape by half closing our eyes as we look at it." Here there is a hint of the impressionism to come.[12] He discovered that physical things transmogrified into bizarre and wonderful shapes under his gaze. As early as his first book of poems he had asked in "Tamerlane,"

> In spring of life have ye ne'er dwelt
> Some object of delight upon,
> With steadfast eye, till ye have felt
> The earth reel—and the vision gone?

Much of his later work is a footnote to this question.

Poe went to romantic philosophy for support of romantic literature. He studied the German idealism called *Naturphilosophie,* which began with Kant and ran through Fichte and Shelling to Hegel. Schelling powerfully influenced Coleridge, and both influenced Poe, who used their thought as a fulcrum from which to smash imaginatively the workaday world and then to rebuild it just as imaginatively according to his own specifications. The creation of the universe and its apocalyptic doom are the subjects of "The Colloquy of Monos and Una," "The Conversation of Eiros and Charmion," and "The Power of Words." Poe gathered together his thoughts and images in "Eureka," which traces the evolution of the cosmos, describes its structure, and anticipates its fate at the end of time. He addressed this prose poem "to the dreamers and those who put faith in dreams as in the only realities."[13]

Poe, following the romantic movement, appealed to art and science, as alternatives to what is usually called reality (but he ignored that other romantic avenue of escape, history, which held no real interest for him).

II *The Shock of Experience*

So far is has been possible to give a fair account of Poe by suggesting that his powerful imagination transformed into fiction and poetry the data given to him by his milieu and his reading. Stopping here, we might be inclined to agree with those who consider him simply a romantic artist in the Gothic tradition, a greater Brockden Brown. "The Fall of the House of Usher" might be explained as we explain Hawthorne's Gothic short story "Rappaccini's Daughter."

Still, Poe's handling of his subjects has a different, more tangible quality that Brown's or Hawthorne's. His superiority is more than a matter of art, for there is a violent realism in his macabre writings unequalled by the other Americans who worked in the same genre. His was no mood of superficial romantic melancholy or dramatic Gothic imagining when he wrote "The Black Cat," "The Tell-Tale Heart," "Ligeia," "The Pit and the Pendulum." There is no escaping the inference that these stories "move" because of the impact of his personal experience, no matter what practical or artistic motives he may have had for writing them.

Despite Poe's affiliations with the romantic movement, he cannot be circumscribed by its definitions. He was never, even in his most immature days, a man of sentiment and sensibility as these terms were defined by the romantics. He never believed in letting the passions run riot. His reluctance to do so was a native quality heightened, deepened, strengthened, darkened, by his very familiarity with the processes of his imagination, which did not invariably convey him to a Platonic Seventh Heaven wherein he might commune ecstatically with transcendent beauty. More and more it ushered him through an inferno no less harrowing for being subjective—private to his own thoughts and feelings.

His imaginative flights were fine—as long as he controlled them. Too often they went not only unguided but in the wrong direction. He, who so frequently appealed to the imagination against the abstract reason, had forced upon him the recognition that his admired faculty was a Frankenstein: Sent in quest of ravishing visions, it might well choose to sport with hideous spectres instead. Poe twice, in "Marginalia" and in "The Premature Burial," warns his readers in much the same terms not to rely on the imagination to ease the spirit when it has been injured by harsh actualities:

> There are moments when, even to the sober eye of Reason, the world of our sad humanity must assume the aspect of Hell; but the Imagination of Man is no Carathis, to explore with impunity its every cavern. Alas! the grim legion of sepulchral terrors can *not* be regarded as altogether fanciful; but like the Demons in whose company Afrasiab made his voyage down the Oxus, they must sleep, or they will devour us—they must be suffered to slumber, or we perish.[14]

Poe's dictum unmistakably bears upon it the autobiographical imprint. When he set it down in writing, he was far advanced in his empirical knowledge of "the grim legion of sepulchral terrors." His imagination had measured the limits of dread in real earnest because the world had battered his soul and left him weak and shaken—and vulnerable to the nightmares that do not wait for sleep to announce their arrival.

Poe passed through the romantic rainbow and came out on the other side as something the romantic poets would not have recognized or understood. He could not have sustained the Bryonic pose because he was without Byron's forceful personality and high determination. He would not have been an American Keats because artistically he was more than an ethereal lyricist. What is closer to the point, he suffered a series of calamities that would have staggered Byron and swamped Keats.

The primal calamity was part of Poe's nature, the native weaknesses that he brought into the world with him. A deadly streak of melancholia possessed him and erupted within his psyche even in the best of outward circumstances, as is proved by one paragraph from a letter written to John Pendleton Kennedy when Poe was fairly prosperous because of his connection with the *Southern Literary Messenger:*

> My feelings at this moment are pitiable indeed. I am suffering under a depression of spirits such as I have never felt before. I have struggled in vain against the influence of this melancholy—*you will believe me* when I say that I am still miserable in spite of the great improvement in my circumstances. I say you will believe me, and for this simple reason, that a man who is writing for *effect* does not write thus. My heart is open before you—if it be worth reading, read it. I am wretched, and know not why. Console me—for you can. But let it be quickly—or it will be too late.[15]

Poe would collapse into such a state off and on throughout his life. His emphasis on the word "effect" is relevant to many of his writings besides this letter. If he customarily wrote for effect, it is no less true that his verisimilitude was often not a matter of literary art by itself, but of literary art utilizing experience—and experience that he suffered in defiance of his will or intention. *He* felt a pathological depression of the spirit before Roderick Usher did.

Poe's nerves were never robust from the moment of birth; he never learned to control them under the pressure of great excitement or crises of responsibility; and he lacked the moral stability to avoid looking for an escape hatch when the pressure became intolerable. Notoriously, he sought the bottle for a companion in his retreat from reality; and the fact that he was no habitual drunkard supports rather than impugns this truth about his character. He asserted in a letter to Sarah Whitman, written about a year before his death, that he drank, not for pleasure, but to get away from "torturing memories . . . insupportable loneliness . . . a dread of some strange impending doom."[16] His statement is correct as far as it goes, but it needs to be integrated into a more general principle: He felt tempted by alcohol in any moment of emotional upheaval, even one of optimism or exaltation.

His unwillingness to accept reality in all of its crudity was vastly exacerbated by another psychological ailment—an almost suicidal wish to act against his own best intersts. Poe accurately summarized the facts about this condition in "The Imp of the Perverse."

> There lives no man who at some period has not been tormented, for example, by an earnest desire to tantalize a listener by circumlocution. The speaker is aware that he displeases; he has every intention to please; he is usually curt, precise, and clear; the most laconic and luminous language is struggling for utterance upon his tongue; it is only with difficulty that he restrains himself from giving it flow; he dreads and deprecates the anger of him whom he addresses; yet, the thought strikes him, that by certain involutions and parentheses this anger may be engendered. That single thought is enough. The impulse increases to a wish, the wish to a desire, the desire to an uncontrollable longing, and the longing (to the deep regret and mortification of the speaker, and in defiance of all consequences) is indulged.

If Poe was not speaking autobiographically here, he should have been, for he had more than a nodding acquaintance with the Imp of the Perverse. It rode the train to Boston with him when he went to lecture before the Lyceum following an invitation from James Russell Lowell. Sure of a knowledgeable and distinguished audience, Poe had much to gain from making a good impression with the new poem he had promised to read. What he did instead was to emote the well-known "Al Aaraaf" and "the Raven"; and, as if this were not sufficient affront to his hosts, he returned to New York and wrote contemptuously that what he had given them was as much as they deserved.[17]

His Imp of the Perverse accompanied him on a more catastrophic venture, his visit to Washington where his friends had arranged a meeting for him with President Tyler. A possible government job at stake, Poe arrived drunk, scandalized those who saw him, obviously could not be presented to the President, and was sent back to Philadelphia in disgrace.[18]

Poe was forever inflicting this kind of compulsive self-defeat. He, who wanted so badly to shine and to be admired, repeatedly created the condition in which he was sure to be pitied, snubbed, insulted, and humiliated. From himself he drew the understanding of compulsions that enabled him to write not only "The Imp of the Perverse" but also "The Black Cat" and "The Tell-Tale Heart."

He was thus a man divided against himself, and it was by looking within, by following threads leading into the depths of his personality, that he learned to write such a story as "William Wilson," which turns on the fact that the main character is haunted and pursued by an exact double, even to the name, who is the incarnation of his own conscience. In the same way Poe could comprehend his "Man of the Crowd" who wanders alone cut off from the throng by some strange psychological barrier. So adept was Poe at self-analysis that at his best he seems to be writing case histories comparable (if we ignore his art) to many in the annals of abnormal psychology.

The seeds of Poe's spiritual malady were cultivated during his infancy. When he was two years old, the father of the family, David Poe, disappeared, leaving the mother trapped in a predicament that might be called tragic or pathetic if it did not beggar adjectives like these. Elizabeth Poe, although still in her twenties, was poverty-stricken, wasted by tuberculosis, caring as best she could for one infant, worried about a second from whom she was separated, pregnant again, and compelled to go out on the boards and play comic roles whenever she could get a billing. Such were the circumstances in which her daughter, Rosalie Poe, was born.

Her elder son, William Poe, stayed with his paternal grandfather. The other two children she kept with her as she toured the theatrical circuit in Carolina and Virginia, struggling desperately to survive, failing with frightening rapidity until her earthly sorrows were finally stilled in Richmond. Her fate was, says Hervey Allen, "one of those petty victories of which even Death might be ashamed."[19] To her younger son Elizabeth Poe bequeathed a miniature of herself, a poignant memory, and the duty of defending her honor in later years. She was the first of the languishing, dying women in his life—followed by Jane Stanard, Frances Allan, Virginia Clemm—who gave Poe a fearful sense of the nearness of death, a subject about which he would write much.

Undoubtedly the mature Edgar Poe referred to his mother so infrequently because he could not bear to talk about her martyrdom. She contributed something to the creation of his young, beautiful, gifted, delicate, doomed heroines like Madeline Usher. Beyond that he avoided the subject of his mother, stopping short with the observation, based on his age when she died: "I myself never knew her."[20] His sonnet "To My Mother" was addressed, not to her, but to his mother-in-law.

The seeds grew in his infancy and then sprouted into monstrous growths as they were watered by repeated misfortunes. Lifted from sordid surroundings when the John Allans took him in, he knew a comfortable life until crushing disappointment hurled him back into the mire, all the more deeply for his having learned what it felt like to be out of it. He accompanied the Allans to Britain; he played the role of a young Virginia aristocrat in their Richmond home; yet, he lived on the edge of the abyss because they never adopted him. Legally he had no redress when John Allan cut him off without a penny.

Poe's year at the University of Virginia foreshadowed the coming catastrophe. He excelled in his studies, but they had to compete with cards and liquor. He was not a real gambler, nor was he a particularly good drinker (later in life a glass of wine would make him tipsy). But he *was* a convivial companion who fell easily into the standard university life of the Virginia gentry, with the result that he soon ran up gambling debts that he could not pay, that John Allan *would* not pay. He had to leave without a degree although he took with him the insight into college ways that he subsequently used in "William Wilson."

Allan has often been blamed for Poe's exile from home; and there is no doubt that he acted unforgivably when, in the course of their correspondence, he insinuated the illegitimacy of Rosalie Poe, Edgar's sister. He had, on the other hand, real cause for anger. He had treated Poe well for fifteen years, and he had not bargained for the return he got when Poe's gambling debts arrived on his desk.

Poe, moreover, was not an easy individual to deal with. He was vain, irritable, easily roused by criticism, and inclined to believe that the world owed him, if not a living, at least an indulgence with his whims. Perhaps so much is understandable in a thwarted genius. What cannot be so explained was a neurotic bent, perhaps inherited from his father, that would make him first react with anger and arrogance, and then, disconcertingly, turn around and beg for assistance. Allan saw this side of Poe more than once.

Allan's sin was to offer a grudging support that helped Poe a bit and encouraged his expectations, but did not relieve his anxieties or allow him to maintain himself in the given circumstances. This situation existed not only at the university but at West Point, both of which Poe had to abandon for financial reasons; and it continued intermittently until the final break between the two men. Poe tried at various times to come to a reconcilation, for he thought he might inherit some of the Allan estate. He failed partly because he was tactless and demanding, partly because Allan would not accept what he should have regarded as a moral obligation toward one who had been in his care since infancy.[21]

The shipwreck of Poe's hopes for financial security was a near-fatal blow to him, for he was utterly ill-fitted to cope with his environment. True, he failed to receive a federal appointment comparable to Hawthorne's in customs and to Irving's in the diplomatic corps; but it may be doubted that he could have made a success of such an appointement had he got it. He sat in the editor's chair of leading literary magazines, and by his literary skill was eminently qualified to do so; yet, he always was forced to move on, whether because of personal antagonisms or because of his unreliability. As early as 1835, when he was on the *Southern Literary Messenger,* a warning sound is heard that will grow ever louder. Publisher Thomas White adjures him: "No man is safe who drinks before breakfast! No man can do so, and attend to business properly."[22]

The terrible irony is that Poe could not make a living at a time when he was known to be a writer of extraordinary ability. He labored indefatigably with his pen, and an enormous mass of his writings, creative and critical, appeared in the journals. He won prizes for "MS. Found in a Bottle" and "The Gold Bug." "The Raven" caused an overnight sensation. He could not, nonetheless, live on what he earned. His America was not one in which literary success would necessarily be rewarded with anything more substantial than fame.

A mirage led him on—the mirage of a magazine of his own. He followed it into one disappointment after another, for his plans for the *Penn Magazine* and the *Stylus* never passed beyond the prospectus stage, while his duties as editor and proprietor of the *Broadway Journal* involved little more than presiding over its obsequies after its financial demise. He never knew security.

At least as great a disaster to him was his unfortunate relations with women, Through his life they file in succession—Jane Stanard, Elmira Royster, Frances Allan, Mary Devereaux, Frances Osgood, Marie Shew, Sarah Whitman, Annie Richmond. In each he sought the aura of the feminine, the idealized abstract Platonic woman whose image he carried inside his head. Elmira Royster rounds out the circle of his fate in this regard. When he was at the university, her father interrupted their romance by intercepting his letters. Over twenty years later, she being now a widow, they met again and arranged to marry at last—only to have death overtake Poe in Batimore immediately afterward.[23]

He too had been married before. He made a lamentable choice, his cousin Virginia Clemm. She was only thirteen, an age so tender that it provoked hostile comment. The argument has been advanced that he preferred his cousin because he did not want the marriage to be a real one; the facts are obscure; we have no warrant to say positively that his attitude toward Virginia was out of the ordinary. In any case he certainly loved his wife an he probably suffered more than she did during the six agonizing years during which she declined, through recoveries and relapses, toward the grave. Virginia may have inspired him to write "Annabel Lee." She certainly gave him his model for Eleonora, the cousin and child-bride of "Eleonora." And she left him heartsick, physically debilitated, and more than ever a prey to despondency and drink.[24]

Of this dreadful domestic tragedy Poe wrote the most harrowing letter ever written by an American. After describing Virginia's cycle of attacks and partial recoveries, he confessed to George Eveleth: "Each time I felt all the agonies of her death—and at each accession of the disorder I loved her more dearly & clung to her life with more desperate pertinacity. But I am constitutionally sensitive—nervous in a very unusual degree. During these fits of absolute unconsciousness I drank, God only knows how often or how much."[25]

His condition was so bad that he felt *relief* at Virginia's passing, for this was at least an end, and he had no more hideous crises to bear on her account. "The fever called 'Living' is conquered at last," as he says in "For Annie." He himself remained "feverish." Shock and hallucinations pursued him more tenaciously. His letters, especially those to women, show ever more plainly the drives of his compulsive neuroses. Toward the end he suffered from an acute attack of persecution mania, and died in a convulsion of delirium tremens after a drunken spree in Baltimore.

The relevance of his pathological psychology to his work seems evident. Considering what he saw for himself, there is no enigma about his interest in madness, neurasthenia, death, fantasy and the dissolution of personality. He was compelled by circumstances to recognize their grim existential import when otherwise he might have treated them in the romantic Gothic fashion as merely good material for a particular type of story—the horror story. That is why he is more than an American Tieck, more than another Brockden Brown.

CHAPTER 3

Return to Reality

ALTHOUGH the lure of poetic romanticism and the force of shattering tragedy obliged Poe to escape into his private universe of dreams from time to time, neither of these causes was relentlessly operative in his life. Ordinarily his psychological stability was such that he could stay within and recognize the bounds of reality, and it is only by selecting one-sidedly from the facts about him that his biography can be written as if he were a case for the asylum. Much of his work would be considered unexceptional in another artist. Poe's signature over his writing is what provokes a search for hidden meanings beneath the apparent ones, for covert aberrations behind supposedly innocent incidents and expressions. The antidote to this type of analysis, with its determined bent toward finding neuroses and psychoses everywhere, is to bear in mind that Poe's life demonstrably reveals many qualities that cannot be expressed by a picture of persistent, undeviating, pathological escapism.

I *Normalities*

Apart from the condition of his nerves, Poe was physically sound until overwork, disappointment, and tension weakened his heart and caused him to develop a brain lesion. From his schoolboy days he had enjoyed outdoor sports. He was adept at swimming, and is said to have set a record for the broad jump. That there was a touch of the Byronic pose in his athletics, he himself admitted. He drew the parallel when he claimed to have exceeded Byron as a swimmer. After boasting that he could have swum the Hellespont, he related one of his early exploits in the James River: "I swam from Ludlow's wharf to Warwick (six miles), in a hot June sun, against one of the strongest tides ever known in the river."[1]

His attitude, at the same time, was more than a pose. He took genuine delight in hiking through the woods and along the beach, a habit of which he made good use for background material in "Landor's Cottage," "The Elk," "The Gold Bug" and "A Tale of the Ragged Mountains." He was not a naturalist cut from the Thoreau pattern; but his eye recorded more of nature than the dim spectral shadows, the dizzy whirlpools and the horrid abysses of his Gothic stories. Ellison of "The Domain of Arnheim" postulates outdoor exercise as one requirement of a happy life.

No perpetual dreamer could have worked as hard as Poe did. Sitting in an editorial chair, he was industrious beyond most of his competitors; not did he wildly dissipate his energy into the wasteland of neurosis, but rather channeled it very effectively toward the end set by himself and his publishers. His practical triumph was sealed by the increase in circulation enjoyed by the journals he guided: the *Southern Literary Messenger* jumped from 500 subscribers to 3,500; *Graham's Magazine,* from 5,000 to 40,000. He had a hard pragmatic sense of what the public was prepared to pay for, and he gave it what it wanted. If he went at every job in fits and starts—boiling energy followed by indifference—he suffered from no such pitiless numbing lassitude as did Roderick Usher.

Poe's career with the United States Army is a good example of his practicality. Following his break with John Allan, he enlisted in the ranks under the name of Edgar A. Perry. Serving for the two years of 1827 - 29, he rose to the grade of sergeant-major, handled the regimental correspondence, and compiled a record so outstanding that his officers willingly gave him the testimonials he needed when he applied for entrance into West Point. His immediate superior wrote of him: "Edgar Poe late Serg't-Major in the 1st Art'y served under my command in H. Company 1st Reg't of Artillery, from June, 1827, to January, 1829, during which time his conduct was unexceptional. He at once performed the duties of company clerk and assistant in the Subsistent Department, both of which duties were promptly and faithfully done. His habits are good entirely free from drinking."[2]

A man who could win such a commendation for his conduct in the deadly humdrum of the military was no frenzied neurotic. Poe was dreaming, thinking, writing poetry in the manner of Byron and Moore. He was also keeping his regimental books, standing guard, surviving inspections.

He liked the army well enough to want to become an officer, a status more in keeping with his Virginia heritage. He received official support from his superiors and financial backing of a kind from John Allan; and, in due time, he arrived as a military cadet on the plains of West Point. Here was the worst possible place for an incipient psychopath. If a man cannot adjust himself to society, the grueling routine of a military academy will surely bring out the fact in the harshest way. It did no such thing to Poe. Not a hint of anything wrong appears until the inevitable financial squeeze when Allan refused him the money he needed to meet his expenses. Poe wrote to Allan: "You sent me to W. Point like a beggar."[3] That was the reason he dropped out. He was expelled from West Point, not because of deficiencies in himself, but because he deliberately violated the rules so that he might be cut loose from an intolerable situation. His action was not held against him at the academy: He was allowed to collect subscriptions among the cadet for his forthcoming *Poems* (1831).

If it be objected that this moral and emotional equilibrium dates from early in Poe's life, the answer is that the basic normalities of his character endured. They showed through his home life as a married man. Even during the appalling days of Virginia's decline, Poe lay under no encompassing blanket of despair or self-pity. Visitors to their home on their placid days came away with an impression of something as near to idyllic as could be expected. Frances Osgood reacted thus: "It was in his own simple yet poetical home that, to me, the character of Edgar Poe appeared in its most beautiful light. Playful, affectionate, witty, alternately docil and wayward as a petted child—for his young, gentle, and idolized wife, and for all who came, he had even in the midst of his most harassing literary duties, a kind word, a pleasant smile, a graceful and courteous attention."[4] This passage refers to the period about a year before Virginia's death, when the mark of her doom was plain to everyone; yet, her husband could be as normal as that when not horrified by her fits of coughing and fainting.

Poe's affection for both his wife and his mother-in-law is a well-known part of Americana. It is important to notice that while his feeling is expressed in the rarefied poetic sentiment of "Annabel Lee" and "To My Mother," it had also an ordinary domestic significance. He was no Bohemian around the house;

and, if he had been always at home, drunkenness might not have been one of his problems. He tried to be neat in his dress; his wants were simple and easily satisfied; his mother-in-law cherished a deep and abiding affection for him.

Poe was not amoral, let alone a moral idiot. He would not permit morality to compromise the autonomy of his art. He *would,* except when he *could not,* whether because of his poverty or because his Imp of the Perverse held him in thrall, faithfully fulfill his engagements. His leaving bad debts behind him in no way contradicts his desire to make them good. He expected to be paid what he had been offered for his work; he did the work to the best of his ability; he kept accounts of what he owed and what was owing to him. He did not victimize others; he was victimized. He barely received adequate compensation for any of his writings, while his masterpieces were stolen from him and the theft hidden by the pittances doled out to him.[5]

He had the Southern gentleman's respect for moderate religion, the typical Virginian distaste for the extremes of scepticism and fanaticism. His religious heritage fitted Poe, who neither attended church very often nor evaded the religious impulses of his own nature. Logically a pantheist, he would not draw the logical conclusion. Instead he offered a tribute to the essence of Christiantiy in "Marginalia": "A strong argument for the religion of Christ is this—that offences against *Charity* are about the only ones which men on their death-beds can be made —not to understand—but to *feel*—as *crime.*"[6]

Of all the normalities in Poe's character, the one with which he is least often credited is his sense of humor. To write amusingly was not, evidently, his forte, nor would it by itself have made him anything but a minor figure in American literature. Nevertheless, a large amount of his work was intended to be humorous; Frances Osgood, in the passage quoted above, styled him "witty"; and so competent an observer as John Pendleton Kennedy believed that Poe possessed the ability to handle the lightest of themes. When Poe asked for advice about how to conquer his low spirits, Kennedy replied in these terms: "Can't you write some farces after the manner of the French Vaudevilles? if you can (and I think you can) you may turn them to excellent account by selling them to the managers in New York. I wish you would give your thoughts to this suggestion."[7]

Since Kennedy was a professional man of letters as well as

Poe's friend and admirer, his judgment is as authoritative as any we have. Whether Poe was really capable of writing farces for the stage is debatable. He certainly was capable, as his publications show, of writing farces for the magazines. He had a genuine gift for being funny in print, and made use of his gift when he turned out "Diddling Considered as One of the Exact Sciences," "Why the Little Frenchman Wears His Hand in a Sling," "Bon Bon," and "The Devil in the Belfry." He enjoyed fooling his readers with things like "The Balloon Hoax," where he concealed his fiction under the pretense of journalistic reporting about a supposed trans-Atlantic flight of aeronauts. He was capable of laughing at himself: "The Facts in the Case of M. Valdemar" is a burlesque of his horrific stories, and the fact that it was taken very seriously by most readers is a warning that Poe is sometimes being funny when on the surface he seems most Gothic. His "How to Write a Blackwood Article" spoofs the technique of composing terror tales so that they might sell to fashionable magazines. He even joked about his fate (poverty) as a seller in the market ("Secrets of the Magazine Prison-House").

Poe's humor does not make a specialty of airy persiflage or drawing-room comedy. His quips are frequently barbed, as is this one from "Marginalia": "In saying that 'grace will save any book and without it none can live long,' Horace Walpole had reference, I fancy, to that especial grace which managed to save so many books of his own—his Grace the Archbishop of Canterbury."[8] Poe's comic stories are not as uproarious as Mark Twain's. Yet by his very defects Poe enters the tradition of American humor and is one of the perfecters of that very American phenomenon, the tall story. "A Predicament" is a tall story in its combination of buffoonery and exaggerated incident recorded with mock solemnity. All that need be said at this point is that humor was part of Poe's character and anchored him, as humor does, firmly in the world of reality.

When he deflected his humor toward society and politics, Poe became a satirist. Disliking Jacksonian America because he was a romantic artist, he disliked it also because he was a Southern gentleman. He jibed at it in "Mellonta Tauta," "Some Words with a Mummy" and "The Thousand-and-Second Tale of Scheherazade." These satires did not spring from any want of partiotism on Poe's part. In protesting against the crude materialism of his era, Poe was just as American as Emerson, Hawthorne, Melville, Whitman and Thoreau, all of whom castigated their compatriots for loving wealth and status too much. Poe did not oppose the betterment of the people, but he did deny that booming vulgarity was betterment. Had he been simply antidemocratic, he would not have been so concerned about such things as education in Virginia.[9]

It is against the background of the South and its problems that Poe's attitude toward slavery must be judged. Like his class, he accepted slavery as he found it, as he was used to it. Not opposed to manumission as such, he evidently agreed with most Virginia gentlemen in the quarter-of-a-century before the Civil War that Southern paternalism was in the best interest of both whites and Negroes. Typically, Poe stuck to his position the more doggedly because of the Abolition movement in the North, which he resented as outside interference in the domestic affairs of his state.[10]

This is not to say that he was right: It *is* to say that the charge against him of having been isolated from his country and its problems is ridiculous. The common claim that he was a dreamer living in a cloudland "out of space—out of time," unmoved by social or political conditions, can be met, and convincingly met, by a simple negative.

Poe is a distinctly American writer. Even his Gothicism refuses to be divorced from Americanism; his leaning toward horror and terror is not "un-American." Speaking of Brockden Brown and the Gothic story, F. O. Matthiessen remarks: "This ability to take the stock trappings of romanticism and to endow them with the genuine horror of tortured nerves has been a peculiarly American combination, from Philip Freneau's remarkable poem 'The House of Night' through Poe to Ambrose Bierce and William Faulkner."[11]

Poe's strength of mind endured to the end, being most apparent in his last great prose work, "Eureka." His interest remained variegated: The year of his death brought from his pen poetry and stories, criticism and satire, fantasy and science. He never so much as brushed outright lunacy despite his momentary hysterical delusions, and he was able to lecture in Richmond with complete self-possession only a few days before his death. He never made any real attempt at suicide, although he offered one very melodramatic gesture, or at least *said* he did, for the sake

of impressing Annie Richmond. And specifically, he never became an opium addict: He may well have tried the drug on occasion, but what he says of it proves that he could not have been an addict.[12] As for alcohol, he struggled to stay away from it, and did not invariably fail.

There is nothing disgusting about Poe. He was not given to the grisly nonsense of diabolism. Necrophilism was strictly a literary subject with him (he had seen too much of death not to feel a grim personal concern with it, but to infer that he ever felt attracted to corpses in the manner of Cornelius Wyatt in "The Oblong Box" is to say something for which there is no evidence whatever). He was no sadist, no masochist, no pervert, no rake. He even went untouched by minor superstitions like astrology and spiritualism.

The most admirable thing about Poe is his resiliency. That his nervous system was weak, that he had a dual nature that tormented him, that he suffered from fits of black depression, that he was drawn to the themes of death and disease for more than literary reasons—these in broad outline are his patent afflictions; and they can be accounted for without much trouble, given his genetics and his experience. What ought to be stressed is that none of them, nor all together, were able to defeat him. He never gave way to despair. Bad as his crises were, he always bobbed up, his sanity returned and vigorous, his resolution restored, his ambition as sound as ever, his industry unimpaired. It betokens an unbreakable grip on reality that he was so resilient in the face of tragedies that might have turned a less high-strung man into a raving psychopath.

If this analysis is correct—and the record indicates it is—then Poe's life can be visualized by the line of a psychological seismograph where the needle travels across the page virtually in a straight line punctuated by sudden abrupt deviations from the norm. He was ordinarily rational, sensible, hopeful, laborious. He suffered from intermittent eruptions of melancholia, alcoholism, shock, hysteria.

His imagination faced in both directions, toward the normal and the abnormal, giving him a permanent endowment in the heightened sensitivity and visionary power of the poet and artist, and reinforcing his nightmares when they came to him out of the darkness.

II *Reason, Logic, Science*

Of all the ties that bound Poe to the world of reality, none was stronger than his commitment to reason and his faith in its ability to know the truth. He was in a certain sense a rationalist. For all his fantasy and dreams, for all his lyrical paean to the imagination as a means of escaping into a more perfect universe, he held tenaciously to rationalism as he understood it. Poe the romanticist sounds very unromantic when he calls reason "Man's chief idiosyncrasy," separating humanity from the lower orders, and therefore possessed of a special dignity and authority.[13]

Poe arrived at his theory after considering the nature and functions of the human faculties, after identifying the powers of the mind and the special competence of each. Naturally he did not have to do all of his thinking for himself. He relied on his reading of Plato and Aristotle, Pascal and Kant, Schelling and Schlegel, Coleridge and Shelley. To the secondhand information acquired through books, he added some thought of his own and produced a synthesis not precisely the same as anything ever propounded before.

Poe's classification of the faculties enters a path well worn since Greek times. "The Poetic Principle" breaks them down into the three major divisions of intellect, taste, and moral sense; and it holds that these bear, respectively, on truth, beauty, and duty. That is, intellect *knows*, taste *feels*, moral sense *obliges*, each being the final court of appeal when its proper object is under discussion.[14]

The three faculties are not, however, absolutely separate in Poe's theory. He finds that there is an element common to all of them: intuition. The idea of this common element Poe got from Pascal, Poe's intuition being much like the faculty that Pascal calls the "heart." Poe was a good student of the French philosopher on this point—good in the two senses of attentive and apt. He realized, as so many romantics did not, that Pascal was no antirationalist, but rather a thinker who strove to unite intellect and feeling in a more profound synthesis than that offered by the older rationalism.

"The heart has its reasons of which the reason knows nothing." This most famous of Pascal's dicta is no defense of irrationalism, for by "heart" he means immediate apprehension of reality by any faculty whatever. Thus he holds that the "heart" grasps the first principles of science as well as artistic beauty and moral obligation. For Pascal, reasoning *about* these facts—the application of logic *to* them—is outside the province of his basic faculty, but intellectual intuition is very much within its province.[15]

Appropriately, Poe quotes Pascal to the effect that "all our reasoning reduces to a capitulation of sentiment." (Pascal's terminology makes "sentiment" a synonym of "heart.") Poe's intuition is not, any more than Pascal's, a matter of uninformed guesswork. It is not a preternatural power or channel for arriving at mystical revelations. It is not inexplicable, although its operations are not in the forefront of consciousness.

Intuition, whether at work in the intellect or the taste or the moral sense, is direct insight, the sudden effort of the soul when it discards the irrelevancies of a problem and seizes on the explanation at its center. Intuition is a subconscious process—analysis that is itself "little susceptible of analysis," according to "The Murders in the Rue Morgue." In a given case, the facts are assembled by the obvious faculties (perception, memory, etc.). Then, in some mysterious way, the subconscious sorts and arranges the data, finds resemblances, analogies, incompatibilities, hints; and finally "sees" the unifying or explanatory principle, all this so deeply hidden beneath the threshold of conscousness that even the genius of analysis often cannot explain why it is that the solution will in a moment of awareness flash into his mind.

If intuition operates in intellect, taste, and moral sense, how does it differ from these? Poe may have taken his answer more directly from Coleridge than from anyone else, but Pascal states Poe's position clearly enough. In any case, Poe's answer is that each faculty has other operations besides direct intuitional insight: Each works at times discursively, circling around a problem in a more or less mechanical fashion, applying rules and procedural methods. For intellect, this process is the deductive and inductive reasoning of the handbooks on logic. For taste, it is the fancy that moves according to the association of ideas. Intellect breaks down into intuition (analysis) and reasoning. Taste breaks down into intuition (imagination) and fancy.[16] Analysis and imagination are therefore one and the same, a point of the highest significance to art and science.

Poe's knowledge of technical logic was limited, apparently

confined to what he found in John Stuart Mill's *System of Logic,* the standard text of the period and still a book of some weight. Poe is very critical of Mill, but he does not survey the field to see if a better alternative could be found, nor does he challenge Mill's factual description of other thinkers.

Poe extracts from Mill the distinction between deductive and inductive logic. Deductive logic consists in setting down premises that are considered to be true and then arguing to their implied conclusions, as in Euclidean geometry. For a definition of inductive logic, Mill, followed by Poe, goes to Francis Bacon, who says that it lies in gathering all the data, sifting them, and deriving from them general truths like the physical laws of the experimental sciences. Mill has his philosophical reasons for objecting to the division of thought into the two branches of Aristotelian deduction and Beaconian induction, but these may be ignored since Poe does not repeat them.[17]

Poe's rejection of Aristotle centers on the question of axioms —those preliminary judgments that Aristotle considers to be indubitable truths, self-evident and therefore in no need of proof, the starting point that all other thought must have if it is to move at all. Such are the axioms of logic as the principle of contradiction ("nothing can both be and not be at the same time and in the same respect") and the axioms of geometry ("the whole is greater than the part," "things equal to the same thing are equal to each other," and so on).

Poe's position on the classical logic is given in "Eureka": "The simple truth is, that the Aristotelians erected their castles upon a basis far less reliable than air; *for no such things as axioms ever existed or can possibly exist at all.*"[18] He puts the consistency of ideas in place of axioms as the touchstone of valid thinking.

Intimations of modern mathematical logic, with its arbitrary axioms, have been read into this assertion—an unwarranted exaggeration. Poe is not discussing abstract systems of ideas in which internal consistency will validate any set of axioms. He is discussing the very basis of human thought, where the denial of permanent axioms is an invitation to intellectual chaos; and his theory is in fact chaotic since he denies the principle of contradiction and yet defends consistency, which is nothing more or less than the application of that principle. One of his main arguments against axioms is that they have changed during the course of history, which is not true of the contradiction axiom; and he weakens his polemic by pointing to outmoded clichés that were never logical axioms at all ("there cannot be antipodes").[19] If Poe had a point in his anti-Aristotelianism, if he saw that the classical logic was not flawless and that the question of axioms needed rethinking, he failed to work out his criticism.

His case against Baconian induction is sounder. Bacon said that the business of discovering the truth was to gather all the facts first and test them in such a way as to eliminate error, after which the truth would remain as a residue. Poe rebuffs this conception of investigation, denying that the mind "crawls" thus when faced with a problem. He holds that the facts become meaningful only when related to a general law, and that the greatest scientific laws have been arrived at by hypothesis drawn from a few facts rather than by a judicial review of all the facts. What Poe says is true. What he does not say, and doubtless did not know, is that Aristotle makes the very same point.[20]

Despite his criticism of deduction and induction, Poe rejects neither of these branches of discursive logic. Realizing their legitimacy, he merely pronounces them subordinate to "the seemingly imaginative process called Intuition."[21] *They* act by mechanical combinations and require noting more than attentiveness and skill. Thus the Q.E.D. of a geometrical demonstration, or the conclusion of a syllogism, falls into place automatically as soon as the premises are understood. An inductive count of objects or events is just as automatic.

Intuition acts by imaginative possibilities rather than by mechanical combinations, and by theories that outrun the evidence. Once a theory has been propounded, the lower faculties come into play—deduction and induction testing the theory for consistency. If no contradictions can be found, if the consistency remains unimpaired, then the theory is true.

Poe's stock example of a great theorist is Kepler, who discovered his laws by proceeding from mathematical patterns to their physical analogies. "Mellonta Tauta" asserts flatly: "Kepler guessed—that is to say *imagined.*" On this basis, and in a scientific context, Poe can hail "the true and only true thinkers, the men of imagination." The same thoughts reappear in "Eureka."[22]

Poe does not deny that science of a kind is possible without imagination. He knew about the mere accumulation of facts and their winnowing, which was the kind of thing he found in a hack work that he edited and partly wrote, *The Conchologist's First Book.* He used mechanical deduction and induction to eradicate all but the correct explanation of the automaton in "Maelzel's Chess Player." Intuition, theory, he argues, is necessary only when a thinker rises to the level of *creative* science.

Poe became convinced of the predominance of intuition when working with puzzles like chess problems and cryptograms. "A Few Words on Secret Writing" deals with codes and ciphers, and Poe attributes skill in breaking them to intuition—"analytical ability"—for which no puzzle is too complicated or difficult. He insists that "human ingenuity cannot concoct a cipher which human ingenuity cannot resolve." When he was editor of *Alexander's Messenger,* he challenged his readers to send in cryptograms, and guaranteed to solve all of them—a feat he claims to have accomplished with the added triumph of exposing one piece of deliberately contrived gibberish.[23]

Poe has been derided for boastfulness about what actually was elementary cryptography, but then he was no professional, but rather a poet, a short story writer, a critic, and an editor who took to puzzles partly because they helped to sell his magazine. His ability, at any rate, furthered his literary work. It was responsible for some of his best fiction. His brand of logic gives a thematic framework to "The Murders in the Rue Morgue," "The Mystery of Marie Roget," "The Purloined Letter" and "The Gold Bug."

In the first of these stories Dupin explains his method of reasoning as an understanding "of *what* to observe" when confronted by a mass of data. Dupin's logic is Poe's: It is the kind of thinking Poe did when he was being serious in "Eureka" and in "A Few Words on Secret Writing." Yet the logic is successful only in detection and cryptography, and the reason can easily be isolated.

The crime story takes place under carefully stipulated conditions accepted by both writer and reader, and verisimilitude exists only under those conditions. We do not object that it is a fantastic coincidence when Dupin, in "The Murders in the Rue Morgue," breaks into the narrator's thoughts by accurately divining a long chain of associated ideas. We do not protest that his solution of each crime is not impeccable because alternative solutions are always possible. Having agreed to play the game by the rules, we abide by the rules. Coming to cryptography, *there* the rules are objective, beyond anyone's control, since the facts are all available, *there* Poe's intuition has proper scope, works correctly, and arrives at unimpeachable solutions.

The trouble is the "Eureka" discourses confidently of creation and divine volition under conditions where the facts, few and mysterious, might well give rise, and have done so in other writers, to entirely different intuitive insights.[24] Unfortunately for Poe, creation is neither a crime story nor a cryptogram.

Since "Eureka" is supposed to be a scientific treatise as well as a philosphical romance and a poetic vision, it is not necessarily compromised by the one vital fallacy—the idea that we may reason confidently from intuitive feeling about creation to the way the universe did in fact come into being. The science may have an objective validity even if the philosophical theology must be dropped overboard.

It is real science, and Poe may be called a "scientist" if the term is restricted to one who, without being a laboratory experimentalist, read a mass of scientific literature, meditated at length about the import of the latest theories, and then formulated his own system. He had as a boy been interested in astronomy and had spent long hours gazing at the moon through a telescope that John Allan kept on his porch. He went through some months of solid grounding in mathematics and science at West Point. Science is blended with imagination in his cosmic romances: "Mellonta Tauta," "The Power of Words," "The Conversation of Eiros and Charmion," and "The Colloquy of Monos and Una."

Against this can be quoted his early sonnet "To Science," which mourns in romantic fashion the death of poetic legends at the hands of unimaginative scientists and concludes with the great lines:

> Hast thou not torn the Naiad from her flood,
> The Elfin from the green grass, and from me
> The summer dream beneath the tamarind tree?

For Poe, however, the case does not stop there. He knew and lamented that unscientific lore, however adapted to the purposes of the poet, could no longer be counted on to move him as in the past. He knew also that science had added a fresh dimension to the imagination by generating romances of its own. His feeling implies more than the tag that "truth is stranger than fiction." He realized that science had gone far afield from the "dull realites" of the purblind grubber of earthbound facts, and that astronomy alone had opened a whole new world to the poet. That is why he calls "Eureka" a prose poem despite its scientific content. In "Marginalia" he even makes the point that a poem on Saturn is a poor limited thing compared to the spectacular facts about the planet.[25] Science, to the man of strong imaginative insight, has given with one hand at least as much as it has taken away with the other.

Of "Eureka" Poe wrote, "I have chosen a broad text—'The Universe.' "[26] Starting with intuitive perception into universal origins, and evidently influenced by Schelling's (and Coleridge's) romantic *Naturphilosophie,* Poe assimilates the broad lines of astronomy and astrophysics as they were known in his day. He mentions masters like Kepler, Newton and Herschel; he uses Laplace's Nebular Hypothesis as a critical part of his cosmogony; he refers to popularizers of science like John Nichol. He dedicates his work to Alexander von Humboldt, the author of *Cosmos.* He fills his pages with current scientific notions without indicating specific sources.[27]

His system is a kind of pantheism, the identification of God with the world. His disclaimer to Charles Hoffman should not be allowed to go unchallenged;[28] for, however much Poe may have disliked the term "pantheist," it applies to him because of the logic of his thought in "Eureka." His logic moves directly forward to this conclusion from the moment he admits an inability to conceive spirit without matter. His mind begins with hard physical objects, rises through the elements to air and gas, continues on into electricity and the ether that was believed to fill space and carry light and electromagnetic waves, argues that the human soul must be a further rarefaction of matter, and declares thought to be matter in action. God is a supremely rarefied matter infusing everything else. Thus all things, including man, are part of the one divine substance. Poe says as much in a letter to Thomas Chivers;[29] and in "Mesmeric Revelation" he makes the same point.

Poe's cosmology is not without ambiguities, but his considered opinion holds the divine substance to be fragmented in creation and waiting to be unified again after the collapse of the universe into the primordial unity from which it began. Poe's intuition tells him that everything began with unity, a state in which all the atoms of the universe were gathered together interpenetrating one another without division, separation, or multiplicity. God then thrust them apart, radiating them out in groups to fill space and to react upon one another.

The atoms are able to join, although not to interpenetrate, because they are endowed with the forces of attraction and repulsion—indeed, according to an old theory that Poe accepts, matter *is* attraction and repulsion. From this follow the scientific facts we know: gravitation, electricity, magnetism, light, even life and thought. The atoms, striving to return to unity, swirl into great conglomerations and form stars and rocks, earth and water, plants and animals and men. Attraction and repulsion are, therefore, the primordial principles of all existing things in the universe.

A number of passages of "Eureka" read as if they had been written with twentieth-century science in mind, just as Poe's remarks about axioms and consistency seem to foreshadow our mathematical logic. His image of the universe beginning with a unity that is hardly distinguishable from nothing can be regarded as a precursor of the expanding universe of De Sitter. He asserts that the universe of stars is limited, and the statement sounds like Einstein's "boundless but finite." By picturing the atoms as eventually destined to return to the unity that will see them disappear as individuals, and creation with them, Poe apparently is talking about what the physicists call entropy, the running down of the universe.[30]

The negative to these suggestions is easy enough to set up. Poe drew on many of his predecessors without naming them, and so he is not as original as he appears to be. Again, it is never safe to read too much into Poe's words. If he speaks about the eventual collapse of the universe as the atoms come together in a titanic apocalyptic fusion of all created things, this is not quite the same as entropy, which, as far as anyone can guess, may well leave the universe in existence, only stationary and sterile instead of, as now, dynamic and populated with living things.

When this qualification has been made, the fact remains that "Eureka" is so interesting in its scientific theories that two Poe scholars, Arthur Hobson Quinn and Marie Bonaparte, consulted two leading scientists of this century, Sir Arthur Eddington and

Professor Edmond Bauer, about them. Both Eddington and Bauer minimized the strictly scientific worth of Poe's cosmology, but each agreed that "Eureka" does show certain foreshadowings of modern ideas that are of interest because they come from one whose genius lay in a field so widely separated from theirs.[31] Emile, Meyerson, the French philosopher of science, speaks respectfully of Poe's theory of scientific intuition.[32] At a minimum, "Eureka" points forward to the revolution of science through more imaginative thinking—to non-Euclidean geometry, Relativity, and the Quantum Theory.

A monograph on "Eureka" would have to account for these points. All that matters here is that Poe obviously was gifted with scientific understanding and pursued science with a realistic grasp of what was happening in this department of the world around him. There is no contradiction in his concern with a pseudo-science like phrenology. Examining bumps on the head for clues to character had not yet been shown to be absurd, nor was Poe the only intellectual of his time who believed there was something in it. Mesmerism was then considered to be a branch of empirical psychology, and it is, of course, under the name "hypnosis," still with us.

As Poe used logic for his detective stories, he used science to give an air of authenticity to his romances. His insinuation of mathematical and physical facts was so skilful that "The Balloon Hoax" was read as a real history of a real event.

III *Art and Craftsmanship*

As indicated above, Poe's interpretation of reason, logic, and science is directly connected with his interpretation of the artistic. The faculty of intuition has, according to his general theory, an aesthetic meaning, for it is in one of its functions identical with good taste, the faculty that appreciates beauty. The intellect, we have noted, breaks down into intuition (analysis) and reasoning; taste breaks down into intuition (imagination) and fancy. Like reasoning, fancy acts by mechanical combinations. Where reasoning applies the (logical) laws of thought, fancy applies the (psychological) association of ideas.

Inferior taste produces inferior poetry, as Poe argues in his review of Joseph Rodman Drake's *The Culprit Fay:* "The truth is that the only requisite for writing verses of this nature, *ad libitum,* is a tolerable acquaintance with the qualities of the objects to be detailed, and a very moderate endowment of the faculty of Comparison—which is the chief constituent of *Fancy* or the powers of combination."[33]

Since imagination acts by insight rather than by mechanical combinations, it can be identified with intellectual analysis. The way Poe himself moves between science and art exemplifies the intuitive process that pertains to both. Having explored the meaning of unity or analogy in the one field, he is able to apply his findings to the other. Whichever way he looks, he tries to work out fruitful patterns—structures that are significant for either truth or beauty.

Poe is able to erect a rational theory of the arts without falling into arid intellectualism because, where he has already said that intuition apprehends consistency in science, he now says that intuition apprehends symmetry in art. In both cases, the quest is for a unifying principle amid a welter of facts. Echoing Aristotle, but taking Schlegel as his immediate mentor, Poe elevates the concept of unity to a central position in his system.[34] God makes the universe to be one; a good poet makes his poem to be one; and so it is for every sound scientific hypothesis or beautiful work of art.

Science and art are distinguishable because, although the same faculty operates, its aims are different, its purposes disparate. Scientific intuition looks for truth that may happen to be beautiful, artistic intuition for beauty that may happen to be true. Scientific intuition breaks up experience into its component parts and reassembles them into a pattern that reflects the true; artistic intuition does the same thing, with this essential difference, that the pattern *it* fashions reflects the beautiful. Without imaginative intellect, science is crippled, and without intellectual imagination, art is crippled.

Poe's classification of the faculties, with the focus on art, may be put thus:

Intellect	→	Truth
Taste	→	Beauty
Moral Sense	→	Duty

If we abstract intuition, the element common to the three faculties, we get the following scheme:

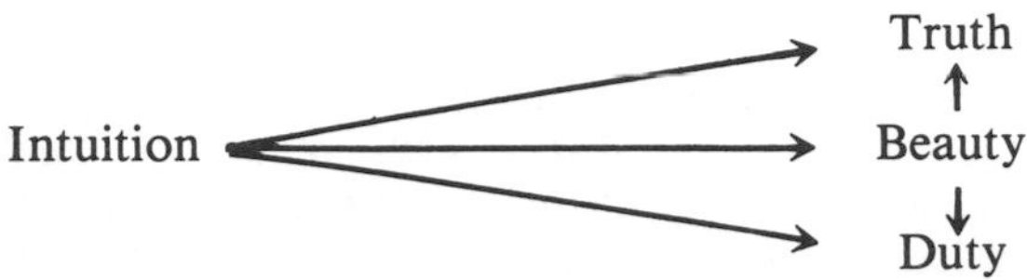

The place of conscience and duty is a question that Poe does not philosphize about. He wrote nothing on ethics comparable to his treatise on science ("Eureka") or his essay on art ("The Poetic Principle"). Nevertheless, in the latter work he links the operation of taste with the moral sense by holding that goodness is beautiful and vice ugly, so that it is proper to look for the goodness in art.[35] His reference is not to anything as simple-minded as moralizing or preaching, but to artistic goodness, to goodness as a by-product of beauty. Poe whimsically applies the sub-title "A Tale with a Moral" to his "Never Bet the Devil Your Head" in which he begins by satirizing those of his critics who were disturbed because they could not find edifying homilies in his stories.

His discussion of art and truth makes his point clear. One of his famous phrases, from "The Poetic Principle," is "the heresy of *The Didactic.*"[36] He means that the artist is concerned with truth in the artistic sense only, in the sense of a by-product of beauty, and not in the scientific sense, so that teaching is ruled out along with preaching. Truth, as a direct objective sought for its own sake, should be left to scientists and other practical men.

When Poe's definitions are thus isolated, there is no possibility of refuting him with his own words because he states: "He must be theory-mad beyond redemption who, in spite of these differences, shall still persist in attempting to reconcile the obstinate oils and waters of Poetry and Truth."[37] Poe is talking here about scientific truth and ethical truth, not about artistic truth. He agrees, or rather insists, that truth is always beautiful, beauty is always truthful, but not in the superficial factual sense. The true and the good discovered by the artist may be very far from satisfying anyone else.

Poe is defending a theory of art that will become after him a whole philosophy, especially in Europe and more particularly in France. It is the theory of the autonomy of art—art for art's sake. Poe opened a door in aesthetics through which many writers, poets, musicians, and painters would willingly, joyfully, pass when he wrote:

> We have taken it into our heads that to write a poem simply for the poem's sake, and to acknowledge such to have been our design, would be to confess ourselves radically wanting in the true Poetic dignity and force:—but the simple fact is, that, would we but permit ourselves to look into our own souls, we should immediately there discover that under the sun there neither exists nor *can* exist any work more thoroughly dignified—more supremely noble than this very poem—this poem *per se*—this poem which is a poem and nothing more—this poem written solely for the poem's sake.[38]

Poe is thinking of art generally and not specifically of poetry. Basing himself on nature ("our own souls") he warns the artist not to corrupt his art by making it the servant of preaching or teaching. This was a point that Poe felt had to be stated as uncompromisingly as possible to offset the contrary thesis of Emerson and the Transcendentalists who preferred to the role of the artist the superior dignity of the seer and the prophet.[39] Poe, who will have none of this attitude, never admits that the artist should defer to anybody: He issues a declaration of independence in the name of art. Recruits have been flocking around his flag of defiance ever since.

Poe's aesthetics and art theory benefited from his denial of axioms. This denial will not do in science, but it will do in art very well. The imagination is released and allowed to fly freely. Cut loose from an unmoving base, the intuition may penetrate anywhere instead of being held in check. It can live, for example, with factual contradictions as long as artistic symmetry is there.

Emerson, always the philosopher, has no such freedom (nor, of course, does he want it). He must bring every fragment of experience, every idea and volition and mood, to the touchstone of his abstract system of thought; and therefore his reactions cannot be wider than his system. Anyone who feels dubious about Transcendentalism as a philosphy is bound to find much of Emerson's prose and poetry defective just because of the persistent projection backward to the premises that necessarily lie behind the conclusions.

Poe can take his starting-point wherever he likes, or, more accurately, wherever his artistic sense permits. By denying fixed axioms but adhering to logic, he is able to produce the *tour de force* of the controlled dream, the mania with a coherent pattern, the disciplined obsession, as in "The Black Cat" and "The Tell-Tale Heart." His intuitive logic can be refuted when its practical truth-value is at issue, but artistically it was responsible for the triumphs of "The Murders in the Rue Morgue" and "The Purloined Letter."

Poe speaks of symmetry—artistic consistency—in a figure derived from science, noting that in either field the joining of elements may add up to something more than the component parts.

> The *pure Imagination* chooses, from *either Beauty or Deformity,* only the most combinable things hitherto uncombined; the compound, as a general rule, partaking, in character, of beauty or sublimity, in the ratio of the respective beauty or sublimity of the things combined—which are themselves still to be considered as atomic—that is to say, as previous combinations. But, as often analogously happens in physical chemistry, so not unfrequently does it occur in this chemistry of the intellect, that the admixture of two elements results in a something that has nothing of the qualities of one of them, or even nothing of the qualities of either.[40]

To be able to find word combinations that produce powerful "chemical" reactions is, in his opinion, which no one is likely to dispute, one of the greatest gifts a writer can have, whether in prose or verse.

Poe's theory of artistic truth permits him to avoid crude naturalism or simple imitation. He considers literal truth, faithfulness to unadorned fact, photographic realism, to be a fatal vice in art. "In my view," he says, "if an artist must paint decayed cheeses, his merit will lie in their looking as little like decayed cheeses as possible."[41] Poe limits painting too drastically, and sounds as if he had never looked at the realism of Rembrandt or Vermeer; but his general thesis is correct, for the old masters of the still life give us *poetic* realism, realism infused with creative intelligence. Of Poe's works, those that violate his aesthetic principle about "decayed cheeses" are the supposed case histories like "Mesmeric Revelation" and "The Facts in the

Case of M. Valdemar," in which artistic failure is the price he pays for a successful hoax. When he adds *artistic* verisimilitude to realism, he achieves the triumph of "The Cask of Amontillado."

What he wants the artist to portray is, not the natural as the senses give it to us, but "the *general intention of Nature*"—Nature in her creative moods.[42] Art is "the reproduction of what the Senses perceive in Nature through the veil of the soul."[43] What he means is that the artist must be an interpreter who adapts his experience to the needs of his imaginative vision and creates his own private universe from the wreckage he has made of the "real" world. The word "creating" exactly expresses Poe's attitude toward the work of the artist. As God creates the universe from pre-existing atoms, giving it being and meaning through a unified symetrical structure, just so does the artist play God with the materials at his disposal; and he approaches the divine activity just in so far as he creates unity out of variety and compels the observer to accept his vision.

"The Universe is a plot of God."[44] It is a scientific plot that man may follow by using his scientific intuition. A work of art, Poe would add, is a plot of the artist. It is an artistic plot that the observer may follow by using his artistic intuition. In science the problem is to uncover the plot, the underlying unifying principle, and then to test it by the facts to be sure that no mistake has been made. In art the same problem exists, the practical criterion of success being the effect on the beholder—whether he perceives the beauty that the poet is trying to reveal, or feels the horror that the writer of the Gothic story is trying to arouse.

Art is rational for Poe, just as the universe is rational. Incoherent art is a contradiction in terms. This is not to deny mystery in either art or science, or to hold that insights may not be partial, fragmentary, momentary. To deal with human experience that goes beyond clear vision is one of the most significant of all the tasks that Poe sets before the artist. The most powerful way of dealing with it is through symbolism.

The introduction of symbols to express truths not amenable to simple statement was a habit of American writers in the nineteenth century, practiced by Emerson, Hawthorne, Melville and Whitman. Poe was, therefore, quite in the American tradition, one of its founders and perhaps it brightest ornament, when he turned to symbolism. At about the same time as Emerson and Hawthorne, he was looking for analogies between man and nature.

"Analogy" is a basic word in Poe's dictionary of art and science. According to his definition, an analogy is a similarity of structure perceived by intuition, a similarity that helps us to get at the truth about the physical universe, or at the beauty of the artistic universe. Poe is writing by analogy when he reasons from trances to death in "Mesmeric Revelation," from sleep to immortality in "The Colloquy of Monos and Una." Dupin thinks by analogy when he solves the mystery of "The Purloined Letter" by inferring the behavior of the criminal from a knowledge of how human psychology operates—by jumping from what *this kind of man* would probably do in a particular situation to what *this man* has in fact done in this precise situation. Poe used the principle of analogy very effectively in "The Fall of the House of Usher" when he compares the mansion and the family, finding an identical pattern in each, and when he makes the events in the book being read correspond to those going on in the house.

Naturally a man of Poe's intelligence could not be unaware of the pitfalls awaiting the seeker of symmetries. He sees the danger of false analogies. "Eureka" warns the reader to beware of the intellect's "propensity for analogical interference," its "monomaniac grasping for the infinite"—that is, of mistaking arrant dreams for explantory theories.[45] The fact that Poe himself is too ready to find scientific analogies where there are none, or none that can be subjected to proof, is what vitiates his cosmology. His aesthetic sense of symmetry usually saves his stories and poems, granting them an artistic truth that leaves factual truth irrelevant. When he fails, it is usually because his artistic intellect is being fanciful, mechanical, rather than imaginative—when it is assembling trivial resemblances rather than strong enlightening analogies. His failure, by his own theory, is to art what reasoning without intuition is to science.

Symbolism is wider than analogy, for one thing can represent another without any bond of structural similarity. Poe treats his symbolism in different ways. Sometimes his symbols are natural or self-evident (Psyche standing for the soul in "Ulalume"). Sometimes they are accepted by convention (the bust of Pallas standing for wisdom in "The Raven"). Sometimes they are Poe's invention (a moth or butterfly standing for the lady's eyes in "Ligeia"). Not all of Poe's symbolism has been deciphered, and his poetry is difficult mainly for this reason. The scholarly disputes about its meaning and its merits frequently have to do with the symbols involved.

Art is for Poe, as for most artists, an asylum from what is called reality. It carries him into a higher reality; it allows him to turn from the vulgarities around him, and to penetrate a realm where all that counts is supernal beauty and aesthetic values. His love of his art, is, in this sense, a matter of escapism.

But in another sense it keeps him within the reality we all know. Any work of art, as a practical product of the artist's genius, and not merely of his aesthetic experience, results from manipulating physical things like paper and pencils and editors. From the intuition of beauty, the poet must descend to the making of the poem. From the intuition of humor or horror, the writer must move on to produce the story of humor or horror.

The artist is a craftsman; and about nothing else is Poe more insistent. In the greatest art he finds meticulous craftsmanship—that is, hard work. Agreeing with Plato and Shelley that inspiration has to be present, he adds immediately that left to itself inspiration is naive and formless; it has to be defined and shaped and worked up into the unified structure that will give it the most telling impact on the observer. To deny this is analogous to maintaining that all science needs is theory, and that the exacting labor of experiment and proof is superfluous. The sequel to inspiration has to be the patient, systematic, intensive application of the intelligence so that the best means may be found of arriving at the desired end; and to say that great art can be tossed off casually by one who does not comprehend exactly what he is doing is to misunderstand the nature of art. "In all cases," Poe asserts, "if the practice fail, it is because the theory is imperfect."[46]

Poe is his own best illustration of his dictum, for there has never been a more disciplined artist. He knew what he was about, and he freely took upon himself the hard work of keeping at his writings until they said what he wanted them to say. His industry was monumental, his dissatisfaction with inferior work implacable. An editor meeting a deadline cannot always be at his peak, but with his major works Poe was continually rethinking what he had done, continually revising, adding and subtracting poetic lines, rewriting his prose. He is a craftsman of an exacting type.

He is an *objective* artist. He takes all of his sources—the romantic tradition, other writers, reports of feats and crimes, episodes he knew at first hand, his imaginative flights, his twitching nerves—and, extracting the "atoms" he needs, proceeds to build the structure of a given work of art. He, as artist, stands outside his ecstasies and aberrations. His visions, dreams, hallucinations, compulsions, he uses as material for his stories and poems. However ravishing or terrifying the substance, the form imposed on it comes from a cool, judicious, rigorous, calculating intellect.

Allen Tate has argued against this thesis on the basis of traditional faculty psychology—the theory that the human psyche is divided into intellect, feeling, and will. Tate claims that Poe suffered from a disintegration of the faculties such that his intellect, his feeling, and his will could never work together. One of the three controlled the other two at any given time, and this personal disharmony, this civil war within his psyche, Poe introduced into his writings: "Although he was capable of envisaging the unified action of the mind through the three faculties, his own mind acted upon its materials now as intellect, now as feeling, now as will; never as all three together."[47]

The consequence, according to Tate's theory, is that in any particular example of Poe's fiction the characters are dominated by the faculty that dominated Poe at the moment of writing. His hypertrophy of intellect causes his characters to think in the superhuman, preternatural, "angelic" manner of those in "The Colloquy of Monas and Una" and "The Power of Words." His hypertrophy of feeling forbids them to act naturally, which explains the welter of weird abnormalities in "Morella" and "The Fall of the House of Usher." His hypertrophy of will gives them an unholy drive to act beyond the human condition, a perversion of which "Ligeia" is the prime example.[48]

There are several reasons for being dubious about this analysis, even if we ignore what we know about Poe's biography and about his methods of choosing his subjects. The psychology is not sound. Artistic creativity does not work in the fashion postulated by Tate's theory, which fails to distinguish properly between the man and the artist.

That any of the three faculties may exercise a controlling

influence over the mind of a human being in everyday life is evident. Just as any person may be carried away by a fit of abstraction, an angry spasm, or vaulting ambition, Poe was carried away at different times by his intellect, his feeling, or his will. His compulsions were so strong as to make him a good subject for investigation into the manner in which part of a fragmented psyche can suddenly and catastrophically assume hegemony over the rest. His hysteria at Virginia's illness, his belligerence when tipsy, his attempts to stand on his dignity when his dignity was gone—these reactions to different problems of his life reveal how completely he could lose his grip on himself. In this sense, "Poe's failure to harmonize himself cannot be denied."[49]

The fallacy lies in applying this analysis to Poe the artist, who, when he sat down to write, was a fully integrated personality—or he could never have written with his consummate skill. One faculty was in control of his psyche at such times: his intellect. But this was a normal, rational, artistic intellect, not the hypertrophied faculty that Tate describes. One definition of sanity is control of feeling and will by a rational intellect, and such was Poe's condition when he was in the throes of artistic creation.

The same conclusion can be sustained by examining the departments into which his writings fall. The most personal are naturally his letters, and in them we find his feelings flowing through his pen more insistently than anywhere else. Criticism represents a higher degree of abstraction, and here there is less of the man and more of the artist. The highest degree of abstraction is that of the poems and tales, where the man vanishes and the artist remains. Poe's writings thus provide factual evidence supporting the psychological argument that his Gothic stories derived from his rational intellect, not from his perverted intellect, feeling, or will.

Even if we set aside this view of the artist, the contention that Poe's damaged psyche is reflected in his deranged characters still cannot be saved. It is untrue that a writer suffering from a psychological abnormality will, as a natural consequence, portray characters suffering from that abnormality. If an artistic creation can be considered a mirror image of anything, it is of the intellect, not the psyche. A man suffering from dissociation of personality is not able to describe his condition unless he rises above it to the point where he can make an acute self-analysis followed by a rational interpretation—unless, that is, he ceases at least momentarily to suffer from dissociation of personality. Mental and emotional disturbances reveal themselves in quite another way, through confused and disorganized writing in which consecutive thinking is lost. No American writer is freer than Poe of this type of irrationality.

It is a *non sequitur* to infer that, because he suffered from compulsions, therefore his writings are compulsive. Valid logic works the other way. Since Poe's writings are not compulsive, they show a sane creative artist at their origin. Poe is *not* Roderick Usher. He is the creator of Roderic Usher.[50]

There is almost nothing personal (except in the artistic sense) in what Poe wrote. He does not indulge in asides or digressions; he never intrudes himself to address the reader in his own behalf; he never gets in the way of the effect. Considering the personal tragedies, psychological pressures, and social hostilities with which he was afflicted, his objectivity is one of the most remarkable phenomena in the history of American, or world, literature. Poe is America's nearest approach to the pure artist, and in that sense he is the sanest of our writers.

CHAPTER 4

Fiction Themes

MOST of Poe's artistic creativity went into his short stories. They constitute his highest achievement. They more than anything else—more than his poetry or his criticism—give him his place in literature. He labored long and arduously at this kind of writing to which he contributed about seventy individual works, two of which ("MS. Found in a Bottle" and "The Gold Bug") won him prizes, twenty or so of which stand among the enduring masterpieces of the short story. His publication of *Tales of the Grotesque and Arabesque* (1840) is one of the great events of American letters.

The short story was, moreover, a type that he helped to define in theory as well as to develop in practice.

I *The Nature of the Short Story*

Poe had several reasons for cultivating brief fiction, apart from the self-evident one that his greatest ability lay in this direction. First of all, there was a market for the short story. The era was one of burgeoning magazines that required copy to fill their pages. Poe knew of the demand from personal experience: During his career he worked on a number of journals, including some of the best. He served as an editor of the *Southern Literary Messenger, Burton's Gentleman's Magazine, Graham's Magazine,* the *Broadway Journal.* As editor he tried to please his public, and he succeeded by printing good short stories (many of which were from his own pen). Intimately in touch with the mass market, he recognized and exploited the prevailing drift in the reading habits of Americans. "We now demand," he considers, "the light artillery of the intellect; we need the curt, the condensed, the pointed, the readily diffused—in place of the verbose, the detailed, the voluminous, the inaccessible."[1]

America he thought in too much of a hurry to stay with three-decker novels or staid quarterlies with their long tales and leisurely observations about the state of the literary scene. Nor did he find an alternative in the newspapers, which balanced the day's news with trivial fiction to be read quickly and as quickly thrown away. Poe turned to the happy medium—the brief but important types of writing, the few pages worth reading and remembering. He turned to the publications best suited to them—the periodicals published neither quarterly nor daily: "The bulk and the period of issue of the monthly magazines seem to be precisely adapted, if not to all the literary wants of the day, at least to the largest and most imperative, as well as the most consequential portion of them."[2] In his review article "Magazine-Writing," he puts the literary claim for the magazine feature even more strongly by calling it "a *very* important branch of literature—a branch which, moreover, is daily growing in importance, and which, in the end (not far distant), will be the *most* influential of all the departments of Letters."[3]

Poe may be suspected of rationalizing when he concludes that the supremacy ought to be recognized of just that type of writing in which he was engaged and in which he excelled. Nonetheless there is substance in his argument, for although America was to produce, and shortly, masterly novels like *The Scarlet Letter* and *Moby Dick,* American writers ever since Poe have specialized in the short story—and doubtless for just the reason that Poe gave, namely, the preference of the American public for reading material that does not take up too much time.

When Poe appeared, the short story was already flourishing in the hands of Europeans like Mérimée and Balzac, of Americans like Irving and Hawthorne. What Poe did was to adapt the short story as a vehicle for a perfected art-form that is uniquely his own; and he did so by applying his theory of aethetics to his literary practice. His short story is a special case of his search for symmetry and unity in art, which here he locates in concentrated effect, or the bearing of every word, line, and paragraph upon the reactions of the reader. The classical statement of the method is to be found in Poe's famous review of Hawthorne:

A skilful artist has contructed a tale. He has not fashioned his thoughts to accommodate his incidents, but having deliberately conceived a certain *single effect* to be wrought, he then invents such incidents, he then combines such events, and discusses them in such a tone as may best serve him in establishing this preconceived effect. If his very first sentence tend not to the out-bringing of this effect, then in his very first step has he committed a blunder. In the whole composition there should be no word written of which the tendency, direct or indirect, is not to the one pre-established design. And by such means, with such care and skill, a picture is at length painted which leaves in the mind of him who contemplates it with a kindred art, a sense of the fullest satisfaction. The idea of the tale, its thesis, has been presented unblemished, because undisturbed—an end demanded, yet, in the novel, altogether unattainable.[4]

The imaginative intuition, the poetic intellect, of the writer must, if he is to be successful, perceive and combine in the right structure those elements that are sufficient to produce the intended effect. In more common terms, he must know how to build a plot. Since he wants unity, which in this case is achieved through bending every element toward the final effect, he must begin at the end: He must decide first the terminal point toward which the whole story moves. Character, by contrast, counts for little: There is simply not enough room to fill in the little details of psychology and physiognomy that come together bit-by-bit in the novels of the twin giants of the early nineteenth century, Dickens and Thackeray.

The incidents of the plot may vary inexhaustibly, but Poe asserts—and this may sound somewhat strange coming from him—that the whole thing should have an air of realism: "The plot may be involved, but it must not transcend probability. The agencies introduced must belong to real life."[5] This postulate loses its strangeness when we examine his stories. He does not introduce the stock characters of the conventional horror tale—ghosts, werewolves, zombies, vampires. The Devil appears only in the burlesque pieces, never as Mephistopheles, the sinister incarnation of evil, the cunning instigator of human tragedies. Angels confine their activities to the cosmic romances. Reincarnation is the theme only in circumstances where there is at least some difficulty in attributing the given effects to any other cause. Poe's most profound explorations of horror and terror are based on very human and realistic phenomena like mad obsessions. This characteristic is a principal reason for the tremendous impact of his stories.

If realism is one of Poe's strong points, so is symbolism. His theory states that prose fiction, like poetry, like any art, may hold latent meanings that can be deciphered only if the symbols provided by the writer are interpreted rightly by the reader. His "William Wilson" presents a practical example of symbolism in the short story, for it turns on the fact that the second personage is actually William Wilson's conscience. "The Fall of the House of Usher" is full of symbolism, and so is "Ligeia."

In line with his philosophy of aesthetics, Poe's theory of the short story rejects crude naturalism or concentration upon moral or factual truth, all of which become legitimate for him only under the guidance of artistic truth. Also for aesthetic reasons, he demands originality in the short story—new combinations producing new symmetries and therefore new beauties. He condemns "the miserable rant and cant against originality."[6] And as always he sets his face against the idea of all-sufficing inspiration from on high: "There is no greater mistake than the supposition that a true originality is a mere matter of impulse or inspiration. To originate, is carefully, patiently, and understandingly to combine."[7]

Poe's conception of the short story is a good one, too narrow to do justice to all writers who have entered the field, but eminently adjusted to Poe's practice. He obeyed his formula, wrote several masterpieces, and caused his readers to feel the pulsating reality of a unique artistic universe—the Poesque universe.

Poe began his career of short story writer in a conventional way. Following in the wake of Boccaccio's *Decameron* and Chaucer's *Canterbury Tales,* to mention only the classical examples, he conceives of a group of men gathering together to entertain one another by each telling a story in rotation. He calls his group "The Folio Club," and their recitals "The Tales of the Folio Club." When he names the members, he makes clear his intention of using some fashionable forms of the short story, and of spoofing them: His role-call includes Mr. Snap, the president, "formerly in the service of the Down-East Review"; Convolvulus Gondola, "who had travelled a good deal"; De Rerum Natura, Esq., "who wore a very singular pair of green spectacles"; Solomon Seadrift, "who had every appearance of a fish"; Horribile Dictu, "with white eyelashes, who had graduated at Gottingen"; Blackwood Blackwood, "who had written certain articles for foreign magazines."[8]

Thus Poe, already in the public domain as an ethereal

romantic poet, now comes forward as a humorist, as a writer of burlesque parodies of both literary personalities and literary forms. Unfortunately his "Tales of the Folio Club" was never published; and, since no list of titles has survived, the experts have had to sift the evidence carefully before deciding which of his writings ought to be included under this heading. Originally there would have been elevėn, corresponding to the club membership. After he started to publish the stories independently, Poe added others—seventeen in all according to a letter to Harrison Hall. Without going into details, we may say confidently that the following titles either certainly or very probably belong: "Metzengerstein," "The Duc de L'Omelette," "A Tale of Jerusalem," "Loss of Breath," "Bon Bon," "MS. Found in a Bottle," "Silence," "Four Beasts in One," "Lionizing," "The Assignation," "Berenice," "Morella," "King Pest," "Shadow," and "Mystification."[9]

These stories are of the first importance in the Poe canon. Determined to maintain interest by making each of his speakers, and therefore each of their stories, different, he begins his career with a sparkling display of versatility that touches on some of the major themes he will follow thereafter. He writes humorous vignettes and Gothic stories. Under humor we find farces like "Bon Bon," burlesques like "Loss of Breath," satires like "Lionizing." He write "Berenice" and "Morella" and "The Assignation" in the fashion of the Gothic horror story. There are fantasies after the writers of romantic idealism: "Silence" and "Shadow." Adventure, terror, hoax and sea story come together in "MS. Found in a Bottle." The surprise ending, in the use of which Poe long antedated O. Henry, appears in "Mystification." The only important fiction of the later Poe not represented in "The Tales of the Folio Club" is the detective story.

These works constitute an astonishing performance. In his earliest venture into brief fiction, Poe reveals a versatile mind, a dazzling imagination, a disciplined knowledge of what he is trying to do, and consummate writing ability. Naturally neither his theory nor his practice has been perfected this early in his career, and half the stories are negligible. The other side of the coin is that "MS. Found in a Bottle" was striking enough to win him a prize from the Baltimore *Saturday Visiter* for the best short story preesented in its competition, which triumph was followed by the greater one of an editorial job with the *Southern Literary Messenger*. Of the rest, "Silence," "Shadow," "Berenice," and "Morella" are artistic triumphs that remain among the best-read entries in Poe's collected works.

The most singificant thing about "The Tales of the Folio Club" is that they show a distinct development in the author's thought and style. He matured at a single bound and won his independence of his sources perhaps before he realized it. Starting out to spoof the writings of others he finds that somehow his genius had taken command of his pen, so that the burlesque becomes transmuted into sober, serious, and great art. "King Pest," which deals with the adventures of two drunken sailors in a plague-ridden city, is a parody of an incident Poe found in Disraeli; nevertheless, it can be read for its own sake as a grim comedy of errors. To "Metzengerstein" Poe gave the subtitle "In Imitation of the German," but it turned into so vigorous a piece of writing that it broke away from this tie, and Poe, recognizing the fact, subsequently dropped the subtitle. If "Berenice" and "Morella" began as burlesques of the Gothic, they sprang to life under the author's creative hand, and embarked on an independent journey through literary history. "Silence" and "Shadow," whatever Poe may have been thinking of when he termed the former "A Fable" and the latter "A Parable," proved to be masterpieces of mood painting, eerie romances that he never surpassed, so effective that their influence moved Maeterlinck when he came to the writing of his own fantasies.

There is in all this a warning about the interpretation of Poe. His mind runs the gamut from humor to horror; he loves hoaxes; his intent is often masked by deliberate purposes or deflected by the creativity of his art; therefore, it is essential to be sure that a proper criterion is being applied to any one of his works. The difficulty may be illustrated by his long tale, or short novel, "The Narrative of Arthur Gordon Pym."

Ostensibly this is a tale of the sea, with Poe pursuing the success he had made with "MS. Found in a Bottle." Pym sails on a whaler from Nantucket, survives a series of misadventures (imprisonment in the hold, mutiny, shipwreck, escape from the natives of a strange island), and disappears in the waste of the Antarctic. The tale has many obvious faults. The prose is sometimes slipshod. When Poe follows the accounts of real voyages, he too often becomes deadly factual; alternatively he gives shockingly horrible details of murder and cannibalism. There are preposterous impersonations. There is no character development to redeem the tale. He ruins the ending by adding a note to say that Pym survived the voyage and somehow made his way back home.

At the same time, "Arthur Gordon Pym" has its great moments. The prose is often masterful. The sea story is developed so well that it may have a descendant in *Moby Dick*. The handling of horror and terror and the perverse ruinous drive could only have come from Poe. The violence of the sea seems as palpable as in "MS. Found in a Bottle" and "A Descent into the Maelstrom." Pym's ordeal below decks—the compound of darkness, dread, mystery, and waiting, waiting—is depicted with an intensity worthy of the author of "The Pit and the Pendulum" and "Premature Burial." The age-old island culture, with its cryptic symbols, will affect Jules Verne and Rider Haggard and the school of science fiction. The final passage of the novel is Poesque to a degree: "And now we rushed into the embraces of the cataract, where a chasm threw itself open to receive us. But there arose in our pathway a shrouded human figure, very far larger in its proportions than any dweller among men. And the hue of the skin of the figure was of the perfect whiteness of the snow."

Portentious symbolism has been read into this tale. Pym's voyage becomes Poe's journey from reality to illusion, or from fact to dream.[10] It becomes a quest for his mother, or for Mother Earth.[11] Such interpretation cannot be ruled out just because Poe once confessed to a conviction that his novel was "a very silly book."[12] His judgments about himself are not always to be taken at their face value. Besides, his philosophy of aesthetics provides for latent meanings in a work of art that the artist may not hold overtly in mind. Since the "chemistry" of his combinations may give rise to effects that he has not foreseen, he is not necessarily alive to all the beauties, meanings, and analogies in the materials with which he works.

Still, if "Arthur Gordon Pym" really is a psychological novel, *that* is the kind of truth that a novelist, certainly a writer as disciplined as Poe, could hardly be unaware of; and from the rest of Poe's works we know that he was capable of making his purpose clear by using appropriate symbols. If there *are* systematic latent meanings in Pym's voyage, and if they *do* represent the guiding thread by which the plot is to be followed, then Poe has failed to make his point; for the critics who reason thus cannot agree on the sense of the symbols so comprehensive in their import.

Perhaps the danger lies in looking for a single interpretation where none is implied. Perhaps Poe put into his longest piece of fiction a bit of everything at his command—fact, hoax, burlesque, horror, fantasy, psychology and symbolism—so that it amounts to a hodgepodge with flashes of genius on every level. Perhaps that is why it fails so completely of his beloved unity of effect, why he never revised it for publication, why he abandoned the novel after this one attempt. Perhaps, in short, he found that he had over-reached himself, misjudged his vocation, when he wrote "Arthur Gordon Pym."

With sound self-criticism, he returned to the short story immediately thereafter. He began to develop the subjects of his "Tales of the Folio Club" with a surer hand, produced his great *Tales of the Grotesque and Arabesque,* and continued in the same path for the rest of his life.

II *Horror and Terror*

If there is more in Poe's artistic universe than horror and terror, these are, as far as his short stories are concerned, the characteristics that seem most prominent and have attracted most attention. His humor and hoaxes, his satire and fantasies, are pallid compared to the throbbing energy of his gruesome and frightening themes. He took a literary genre with a very high mortality rate—the Gothic tale—and transformed it into something alive and lasting. Who reads William Beckford's *Vathek,* Horace Walpole's *Castle of Otranto,* or even Mary Shelley's *Frankenstein?* Who has not read "The Tell-Tale Heart," "The Pit and the Pendulum," "The Fall of the House of Usher"?

Poe's scope is narrow, but he has remarkable success in avoiding monotony by subtly varying the treatment of stories that resemble one another. He cannot paint his characters fully. According to his stated principle, he does not have to since the unveiling of character is the function of the novel. On the other hand, while his women are much alike (each is his ideal woman in whom traces of his mother and his wife may be found), his men reveal marked differences even in quite brief introductions. William Wilson in flight from himself could not be mistaken for the crazed narrator of "The Black Cat," or paranoic Metzengerstein for Montresor, the sly sadist of "The Cask of Amontillado."

Poe's narrowness is like that of a sword, not that of a bottleneck: it is effective rather than constricting. Nothing adventitious is in his great stories, only the essentials, the minimum of characterization, plot, and atmosphere. By ridding himself of everything except what is precisely to the point, he achieves his unity of effect.

Poe, by deliberate choice, is not a moralist in his fiction. Morality can be found in the tales; for, as he has himself told us, goodness and truth are by-products of art. Since words loaded with ethical content are scattered through his pages—"evil," "wickedness," "vice," "turpitude," "dissipation," "profligacy," "debauchery," "cruelty"—a distinction between right and wrong is implied. Moreover, vicious characters tend to come to a bad end. In "Metzengerstein," pride has a fall; in "The Masque of the Red Death," an attempt to hide from a suffering world leads back to it; in "Hop-Frog," brutality is punished. The reader may accept these endings as a triumph of good over evil. Nothing in the stories forbids him to do so: they are neither immoral nor amoral.

Poe writes, nevertheless, from the standpoint of psychology rather than ethics. It is nearly impossible to condemn sin and crime in Poe's universe as vices that spring from the rational will of a responsible human being. The terrible deeds that abound there result form the pressures of abnormal psychology—from neurasthenia, hallucinations, neuroses, and psychoses. Remorse is always a compulsion, never the self-accusation of a stable conscience after a free and deliberate act. Poe's characters are so far from normality that none should be forced to plead to an indictment in a court of law. The narrator of "The Black Cat" will stand on the gallows, but we know that he should be in an asylum for the criminally insane. William Wilson is haunted by his conscience, but this story is a doppelgänger drama—about the terrifying double of oneself so popular in German literature—rather than a morality play. While "The Pit and the Pendulum" sees the Inquisition defeated, the real ending is the victim's escape after all his agonies and terrors.

Even Poe's detective stories are not moral tales. In "The Purloined Letter," the puzzle is self-contained, and it just so happens that the solving of the puzzle (the finding and retrieval of the letter) leads to the righting of a wrong (the return of the letter to its owner). In "Thou Art the Man," the murder is postulated to start the action, which turns of "the enginery," as Poe calls it, by which the murderer is startled into a confession.

The rest of Poe's fiction can be tested in the same way. He has created a universe, given it psychological laws without denying the existence of the moral law, and peopled it with characters appropriate to such a universe. Other artists have also created strange universes where normality does not apply, where the only question is whether they have succeeded artistically. Poe's universe works artistically.

The reader looking at the world of the tales from the outside can see many a moral that the protagonists, living in that world and controlled by its laws, do not or cannot see. This verisimilitude is Poe's achievement. Putting overt morality out of bounds helps to give him his uniqueness. To condemn him is to miss the point since it is asking him to be a different writer than he was. It is asking him to approximate to Hawthorne, when his greatness is precisely in being what Hawthorne was not. It is wishing that we did not have the stories that Poe alone was capable of adding to modern literature.[13]

In his Gothic fiction, Poe handles the morbid and frightening subjects with which his reputation is so closely associated—death, madness, disease, the dissolution of personality, the wasting away of fragile heroines. Sometimes the incidents recounted are realistic: "The Assignation" tells of suicide in luxurius apartments above the moonlit lagoon of Venice; "The Oblong Box" is about a man driven out of his mind by grief and clinging to the corpse of his dead wife. At other times the uncanny creeps in: "Metzengerstein" features a spectral horse; "MS. Found in a Bottle," a ghostly ship; and "The Masque of the Red Death" is an allegory in which Death is one of the *dramatis personae.* Yet again, Poe's habit is to blend the natural and the weird by postulating hidden but rational laws that govern the action. In "The Oval Portrait," by some occult process the act of painting draws life from the sitter and transfers it to her image. In "The Fall of the House of Usher," the tragedy is so far from being either gratuitous or a matter of capricious volition that both family and mansion are foredoomed to destruction.

Poe liked "Ligeia" best of his Gothic stories.[14] He was probably at fault in his judgement, but it is certainly one of the best. It resembles "Morella" and "A Tale of the Ragged Mountains" in being a story of reincarnation, of how a soul can enter another's body. Ligeia, one of Poe's typical heroines, is beautiful, emaciated, dying; but she also has a preternatural strength of will. The plot turns on her unwillingness to stay dead—"unwillingness" defined in its literal sense. When her husband remarries, Ligeia returns spiritually, poisons the second wife, takes possession of her dead body, and rises from her bier. For all its artistic merits, "Ligeia" remains unsatisfactory because it ends with the husband-narrator at the feet of the reincarnated corpse, leaving the reader to guess what could possibly have taken place between them thereafter.[15] "Morella" ends with the reincarnation in the tomb, and something similar should have been done with "Ligeia." Otherwise, the plot is strong and successful.

Mystery is related to psychology in Poe's works. He finds the interplay of the parts of the soul a subject that can be invested with weird overtones of the faculties are seen, not as cooperating in the normal way, but as involved in a turbulent psychological civil war. One of his key thoughts concerning this topic is about the dissolution of personality. "The Imp of the Perverse" describes a tyrannous impulse warring on the rest of the soul, compelling it to do what the other faculties say should not be done. The protagonist of "The Man of the Crowd" is anxious to join in human fellowship, and unable to do so for some contrary and overriding motive buried in the depths of his psyche. He is almost a foreshadowing of the individual dehumanized and lost in the mass, of whom twentieth-century authors have written so frequently.

The finest thing Poe ever did along these lines is "William Wilson." This is a man's struggle with his conscience, which is allegorized, objectified in another man of the same name and appearance. William Wilson, who meets his conscience first at school, spends the rest of his life trying to evade it. Wherever he goes, whatever he does (and he does some very vicious things), his counterpart inevitably catches up with, and exposes, him.

This "spectre" pursues him from school to Oxford, Paris, Vienna, Berlin, Moscow. Finally, during carnival time in Rome, William Wison turns upon his tormentor. He corners the second William Wilson, stabs him to death—and realizes too late that he has murdered his own conscience, and therefore ruined himself.

Robert Louis Stevenson apparently had "William Wilson" in mind when he wrote "Doctor Jekyll and Mr. Hyde," which also bifurcates a man according to his good and evil tendencies. The psychological fiction that Poe did so much to create has a long history from his time, affecting among others Dostoevski in *Crime and Punishment,* and James Joyce and stream-of-thought novels like *Ulysses.*

The dissolution of personality theme cuts into complicated psychology. Elsewhere Poe studies the mind, not when it suffers from an anarchy of its faculties, but when it is under the tyranny of some one element, one idea or obsession. He enters the field of the starkly, almost clinically, realistic investigation of men who, although they may feel uneasy about their mental states when their tension lets up, are too far gone to understand their mania, let alone to control it.

"Berenice" set the pattern for the later stories of the same type. Egaeus commits the hideous act of opening the grave of Berenice and pulling out her teeth. Yet he knows nothing about it since he is in a state of shock and trance at the time. Since Berenice is said to have been buried alive and therefore to have been the victim of a ghoulish mayhem, Poe was criticized for attacking such a subject; and he admitted, possibly only half in earnest, that he too considered that he had been excessive in trying for a shock-reaction among his readers.[16] He promised to stay within bounds, and did so with "The Tell-Tale Heart" and "The Black Cat."

Each of these has a horrible obsessive murder for its theme, and each follows the development of the theme step by step with a realism that, barring the writing genius, might be a case history from twentieth-century psychiatry. Those who deny realism to Poe cannot be very familiar with our daily newspapers, which periodically carry true stories of murders commited under just such abnormal psychological pressures as those described in "The Tell-Tale Heart" and "The Black Cat."

These two stories demonstrate how varied Poe can be within narrow limits. The former is a direct account by a maniac of how he committed murder because of a delusive compulsion, carefully concealed the crime, and then was driven by a further thrust of his compulsion to reveal it to the police. "The Black Cat" portrays a maniac wavering in his attitudes, killing his wife in one insane paroxysm, when what he really hates is his cat, and causing the truth to come to light by an insane act of bravado. The first murderer seats the police over the grave of his victim, and is exposed only because his rising mania makes him give himself away. The second murderer taunts the police by rapping on the wall where his wife is buried, and is exposed by the wail of the cat that he has inadvertently walled up with her.

If these stories represent realism to the utmost degree, Poe knows how to use other kinds of realism. "The Pit and the Pendulum" has for its central figure a man who is no psychopath, but rather one whose sanity is a necessary ingredient of the plot. Because his mind is whole and his senses keen, he feels sweating terror as he watches the dreadful pendulum descending toward him from the ceiling; if he were in a state of shock, he would be incapable of his subsequent exploration of his cell, following his escape from the pendulum, that leads him to the brink of the pit from which he is snatched back by his rescuers.

Poe's gem of realism—not his best story because its dimensions are too small, but perfect within its format—is "The Cask of Amontillado." Finely-wrought, tight, neat, with no loose ends or superfluities, it strikes with tremendous force within the space of some five pages. Since Montresor is without a conscience, there are no doubts, hesitations or second thoughts to impede the narrative. We do not even know his motive, nor do we need to. It is sufficient that, committed to revenge, and to a certain kind of revenge, he, with the frigid intelligence of an Iago, with the open-faced cunning of a confidence man, entices Fortunato into the vaults, chains him to a wall, and proceeds to entomb him alive. The brutal directness of the treatment reminds us of the *verismo* that Ernest Hemingway brought to his celebrated short story "The Killers." On the other hand, "Hop Frog," another story of revenge, has no such realism: It is laid in a Gothic court, and the revenge of the hunchback on King and courtiers in a body is too excessive to be believed.

Poe's use of symbolism in his Gothic stories is a guiding thread to his literary art. That he is not persistently a symbolist is one of his strengths, for it means that he only turns to symbolism when it has a distinct role to play, and then he handles it with great care to keep it from becoming diffuse or ambiguous. Thus his allegories in "William Wilson" and "The Masque of the Red Death" are the more impressive just because of his expressed distaste for allegory, which held him in check.[17] Allegory never controlled his pen as it did Hawthorne's.

Poe's symbolism generally takes the form of allowing some object to stand for an abstraction or a personal attribute. The clock in "The Masque of the Red Death," with its hourly peal of the chimes, gives to the revelers a promonition that the end for them comes ever closer. Occasionally Poe's analogies play him false; thus the narrator of "Ligeia" finds in the world too many analogies to Ligeia's eyes—vines, butterflies, running water, stars, music, and so on. The handling of the symbols here is crude for Poe: The narrative is clogged by a mere catalogue of objects.

At his best Poe's symbolism is almost faultless, and he is at his best in "The Fall of the House of Usher," which is perhaps the finest thing Poe ever wrote. The symbolic analogies reinforce one another in a steely web of causes and effects. The Usher family and the Usher mansion are analogous—stained with time, used up, crumbling from within, awaiting collapse. Roderick Usher and his sister Madeline, identical twins, are almost two faculties of the same soul, and they can be interpreted together as the soul of which their mansion is the body. All three decline together, and the inference is that the disappearance of one means the disappearance of the others, which in fact is what comes to pass.

After Madeline has been entombed alive for some days, her return to her brother's study is orchestrated by a very clever device, the reading aloud of a legendary tale, the plot of which describes precisely the sounds she makes as she draws near. The door swings open, Madeline collapses against her brother, and they fall dead to the floor together. The narrator escapes just in time to look back and see the House of Usher disintegrate and slide beneath the waters of its tarn.

"The Fall of the House of Usher" is a mosaic of incidents, psychological attitudes, symbols, all cemented into place in a unified structure according to the prescription of an exacting and skilful art. Poe's theory of the short story demands unity of effect, and here he achieves it as nowhere else. He sustains the atmosphere to the end after his justly celebrated opening: "During the whole of a dull, dark, and soundless day in the autumn of the year, when the clouds hung oppressively low in the heavens, I had been passing alone, on horseback, through a singularly dreary tract of country; and at length found myself, as the shades of the evening drew on, within view of the melancholy House of Usher." The concluding line matches the opening in visual imagery. The narrator, looking back, sees the moon shining through a crack in the mansion's wall: "While I gazed, the fissure rapidly widened—there came a fierce breath of the whirlwind—the entire orb of the satellite burst at once upon my sight—my brain reeled as I saw the mighty walls rushing asunder—there was a long tumultuous shouting sound like the voice of a thousand waters—and the deep and dank tarn at my feet closed sullenly and silently over the fragments of the House of Usher."[18]

Poe specializes in great openings and great endings. As always, variety is one of his strong points:

> True!—nervous—very, very dreadfully nervous I had been and am; but why *will* you say that I am mad? ("The Tell-Tale Heart").
> Horror and fatality have been stalking abroad in all ages. Why then give a date to the story I have to tell? ("Metzengerstein").
> I was sick—sick unto death with that long agony; and when they at length unbound me, and I was permitted to sit, I felt that my senses were leaving me ("The Pit and the Pendulum").
> The thousand injuries of Fortunato I had borne as I best could, but when he ventured upon insult I vowed revenge ("The Cask of Amontillado").

There are two peculiarly arresting attributes in Poe's short stories—atmosphere and the description of mental states. The tricks of creating atmosphere he largely derived from the tradition of the Gothic tale: He pruned and tightened and in part augmented what he found in earlier writers. But the description of mental states is virtually his own creation, something he worked out by consulting his own psychology. That is the secret of his understanding. His ability to put this understanding to work in literature is the mystery of his genius.

No one has ever surpassed him, and few have ever equalled him, when it comes to an analysis of emotion washing across the soul like the ebb and flow of the tide. There is an undulation of terror in the soul of William Wilson, Roderick Usher, and the prisoner of "The Pit and the Pendulum." Obsessive fury rises, falls, and rises again, mounting to a crescendo, in the deranged brains of the homicidal maniacs of "The Tell-Tale Heart" and "The Black Cat." When Ligeia returns from the dead to seize upon the remains of her successor, the reincarnation takes place after a series of quivering palpitations in the corpse, after a series of nervous shocks suffered by the husband.

Much of Poe's success comes from his ability to suggest rather than to say outright. How to handle vertigo and trance in a narrator offers self-evident problems. Here is how Poe makes the narrator of "Berenice" speak of his experience: "I found myself sitting in the library, and again sitting there alone. It seemed that I had newly awakened from a confused and exciting dream. I knew that it was now midnight, and I was well aware that since the setting of the sun Berenice had been interred. But of that dreary period which intervened I had no positive—at least no definite comprehension. Yet its memory was replete with horror —horror more horrible from being vague, and terror more terrible from ambiguity." No one could construct a more plausible bridge between two periods of consciousness, and arching over a frightful horror committed in between.

To praise Poe's art of the short story is not, of course, to deny that he has his defects. His prose style is not always impeccable. Horror and terror are themes that too readily lead into the ludicrous; and, although Poe knew as much and capitalized on it in his burlesques, even some of his best things suffer from it. His drama occasionally slips into melodrama, as in "The Pit and the Pendulum" when the walls of the dungeon are brought together mechanically to force the prisoner into the abyss. William Wilson does not sound very convincing when he informs us: "From comparatively trivial wickedness I passed, with the stride of a giant, into more than the enormities of an Elah-Gabalus." Every reader of Poe must decide for himself whether statements like this are hyperbolical or simply absurd.

Of the best of Poe there can be no question. Reading his greatest horror stories is an experience that anyone would be the poorer without, for Poe has constructed a universe to which there is nothing comparable in any literature. He has not cast his net widely over reality, but he *has* cast it deeply, and it *does* plumb reality. He has a right to expect originality of the writer: If he borrows his material from many sources besides his inner life, he gives to it a vitality that it has nowhere else.

III *The Detective Story*

Graham's Magazine carried in its issue of April, 1841, a short story entitled "The Murders in the Rue Morgue." Nothing quite like it had ever been seen before. The reading public was accustomed to tales of crime, whether fictional or of real events, and the violent deaths of Madame L'Espanaye and her daughter would not have been a cause of any particular note, except possibly for protests over the shocking details. What *was* of note was the novel manner in which the author treated his subject. With "The Murders in the Rue Morgue" Poe became the only American ever to invent a form of literature. He invented the detective story.[19]

He also perfected it. This first detective story may be the best ever written. Only "The Purloined Letter" challenges it for that accolade, making the two together the high point in the history of crime fiction. The Poe standard slips with "The Mystery of Marie Roget," which is too long and too involved to hold the attention of the reader. "Thou Art the Man" is better, and represents one critical step forward in the handling of psychology in the detective story. "The Gold Bug" is a superior product by any definition: It helps to establish the wider category of the mystery story—the category that will be expanded by Wilkie Collins and Robert Louis Stevenson.

While fashioning the detective story, Poe came to regard it as an exception to the rule that truth is not the object of literary art.[20] He considers it to be a puzzle in which the object is the correct solution, so that it resembles a cryptogram. His argument needs to be qualified. As his own practice reveals, the detective story is much more than a puzzle and is read at least as much for artistic presentation as for the intellectual manipulation of evidence. That is why the great detectives, Sherlock Holmes pre-eminently, have eclipsed their cases. A cryptogram loses its interest when it has been solved, but a good detective story stands re-reading.

According to the classical rules of detective fiction, three elements are necessary for success, the art of the writer being to unite them properly into a coherent and, within the rules of the game, convincing account. These elements are the crime, the detective, and the method of detection. All three are identified and defined by Poe in one sweep of his genius. His practice is so good that it unnecessary to go beyond him to see how a detective story ought to be written.

The crime is the reason for the story, the cause of the incidents that follow. If verisimilitude is to claim the reader, persuading him to withhold his disbelief and to enter into the spirit of the story, the crime must not shock his credibility too much. He must be not only convinced that there is a puzzle worth unraveling, but also carried along by the narrative until the explanation is given to him. Puzzle without crime Poe deals with in "The Gold Bug," which concerns the discovery of pirate treasure after the decipherment of an old map by using the cryptography of which Poe was so fond. Puzzle with crime produces the detective story, and Poe is no less credible in "The Murders in the Rue Morgue" and "The Purloined Letter" than he is in "The Gold Bug."

The discovery that Mme. L'Espanaye and her daughter have been murdered amid mysterious circumstances starts "The Murders in the Rue Morgue" on its way. The crime has happened on the fourth story of a Paris building. The bodies of the women have been fearfully mutilated, that of the mother thrown into the yard, that of the daughter thrust with tremendous force up the chimney. No one saw the murders or murderers, but several witnesses say they heard voices in the apartment. All agree that one was the voice of a Frenchman; but about the second voice they disagree. A French witness thinks the accents were Spanish; a Dutchman thinks they were French; and Englishman, German; a Spaniard, English; an Italian, Russian.

Who could have had the agility to climb to a fourth story apartment, the ferocity to attack two women so horribly, the strength to thrust one corpse up the chimney? Who was it that spoke so strangely that everyone within earshot feels sure that he was speaking a strange tongue?

The crime and the circumstances of "The Purloined Letter" are completely different. In it the causal situation is theft, the thief is known, and the problem is to retrieve what he has stolen. The criminal is a minister of the Paris government, who, during a visit to the royal apartments, sees an incriminating letter lying on the table. He takes it, knowing that the lady to whom it is addressed cannot protest because of the presence of a third party from whom the letter must be concealed. The police are ordered to find the letter and get it back without letting the thief know what they are doing. Because the authorities are certain that he keeps it in his possession, possibly on his person, their agents, disguised as thugs, hold him up on the street and search him. Meanwhile crime experts, while he is out of the way, go over his rooms inch by inch, probing the furniture, the walls, and every conceivable hiding place—all to no avail. So the puzzle is this: The letter must be on the premises of the thief; the premises have been ransacked, ceiling to floor, wall to wall; the letter is there—but where is it?

When the crimes of "The Murders in the Rue Morgue" and "The Purloined Letter" have been described, when the authorities have admitted failure—at this point every detective story fan since Poe's time has known what the next step is. The detective has to brought into the case. His name is legion: Sherlock Holmes, Philo Vance, Charlie Chan, Father Brown, Ellery Queen, Perry Mason, Inspector Maigret, and so on *ad infinitum.* These are all aliases. His real name is C. Auguste Dupin, who steps forward into modern literature in "The Murders in the Rue Morgue." He has been with us ever since.

Dupin is a gentleman of leisure, reduced in circumstances but not so far as to require that he work for a living. He dabbles in literature and even writes poetry. He has his peculiarities, such as a preference for darkness that leads him to shutter his room during the day, and to go out into the city only at night. He smokes a meerschaum. He knows the annals of crime; and, although a recluse who discourages visitors, he has repeated visits from the highest officials of the police, who reveal to him the facts surrounding certain vexing crimes that have them baffled.

Does it all sound familiar? It should. The more you examine C. Auguste Dupin, the more does the figure of Sherlock Holmes appear in him. Dupin and Holmes even have in common certain minor tricks of their trade: Both, for example, know how to flush out a criminal by means of a newspaper advertisement. We know more about Holmes because Conan Doyle has described him through dozens of stories. Yet Poe has already set the pattern of getting the detective to solve more than one case, and of having him refer back to those that have gone before. Dupin is too strong a character to be held within Poe's limits of the short story, although his personality does not overbear incident as Holmes' does. Literature is full of human types that grew, almost by a natural growth, beyond the intentions of their authors. We know that it happened with Doyle. It seems to have happened with Poe. "The Murders in the Rue Morgue" and "The Purloined Letter" are not merely good plots leading up to effective endings. They are notable for characterization too. C. Auguste Dupin is the eternal detective.

Everything in the detective story depends on the detective, but there are subsidiary interests. Sherlock Holmes must be balanced by Doctor Watson, a fact that Poe was the first to see. Dupin has a companion, the narrator who plays the part of the listener, the man of middling intelligence who must be enlightened about what is happening, and who thereby passes the necessary information on to the reader. He is the link between the detective and the reader, and in his inability to comprehend the meaning of the clues both flatters the reader and shows off more brilliantly the sagacity of the detective. Holmes says to Watson, "You see but you do not observe." He had in mind that passage in "The Murders in the Rue Morgue" where Dupin tells the narrator: "The necessary knowledge is of *what* to observe."

Holmes enjoys a special standing with Scotland Yard. Before him Dupin had been related in the same way to the French Sûreté. The reason for this is that the ineffectiveness of ordinary police methods must be shown, from which follows the appeal of the authorities to the detective to help them. Holmes is approached periodically by Inspector Lestrade, who knew how Dupin had been approached by the Paris Prefect.

Ordinary police methods having failed, the question is what method of his own the detective will bring to the solution of the crime. Holmes calls his method "deduction"; Dupin calls *his* "analysis." They are not very different, for each involves an insight into the pattern of the crime and a correct reading of the clues. Holmes, upon inferring Watson's chain of thought, even mentions Dupin's similar achievement as the basis of this blend of logic and psychology. The manner of reading clues was not original with Poe, who knew the passage on "detection" in Voltair's *Zadig.*[21] Poe's contribution was to raise the method to the level of a regular technique applied by a detective to the solution of a crime.

Dupin wields the imaginative perception of meaningful symmetries that Poe says elsewhere is the key to both science and art. Intuition, acting amid a welter of clues, sets aside the trivia and fastens on a structure that emerges from putting the essential facts together. Then the intelligence may go to work in a more ordinary way, proving by deduction and induction that the solution thus arrived at is the true one—that the man apprehended is indeed the criminal in the case.

What is needed is the imagination of the poet and the reasoning power of the mathematician. The thief of "The Purloined Letter" successfully hides the letter from the police because he is both a poet and a mathematician. Dupin is able to find it because he too is both a poet and a mathematician. Dupin perceives that such a mind, confronted with the task of fooling the experts who will search his apartments in the most exhaustive way, must arrive at the conclusion that the safest way to hide the letter is to put it in a place so obvious that they will not even consider looking there. Hence Dupin, gaining an entrée, finds the letter just where he expects it to be—in the letter rack.

The horrors of "The Murders in the Rue Morgue" fall into place when Dupin realizes that the salient clues—agility, strength, ferocity, and strange gibberish—can only fit an ape. He then deduces from various other clues that the second party probably is a sailor from a Maltese ship, and entices him into coming forward by advertising that a captured orangoutang will be returned to the owner if he claims it. The sailor's confession is the empirical evidence proving Dupin's insight and logic to be sound.

Dupin doubtless was a cryptographer by avocation. Legrand of "The Gold Bug" turns to cryptography in a pure sense when he finds the tattered, weather-beaten pirate map. His method of decoding it would be simply another of Poe's examples of how to break codes except that Legrand uses it very practically to find the treasure hidden long ago by Captain Kidd. One may wonder whether the discovery really could be made in this way, but there is no dipute about "The Gold Bug" being a rattling good story. It deserved the prize it won from the *Dollar Newspaper* of Philadelphia. One of its offspring is Stevenson's *Treasure Island.*

Another of Poe's detective stories in which Dupin does not appear deserves mention—"Thou Art the Man." This is not one of his best (it is too melodramatic for that), but it advances the detective story in one cardinal way: It makes the villain of the piece, not some glowering thug or admittedly amoral gentleman, but precisely the jolly, frank, professedly aghast, friend of the victim. From there it was but a step to the sophisticated modern crime novels which conceal the criminal because he is indiscernible among the group of ordinary people.

Crime fiction is now so common that we can hardly imagine the literary scene without it. We naturally assume that every year will bring astronomical sales of Conan Doyle, S. S. Van Dine, Dorothy Sayers, Agatha Christie, G.K. Chesterton, Erle Stanley Gardner, Rex Stout, Ellery Queen, Simenon, and the hopeful newcomers who keep invading the mystery field in droves. The fiction writer is rare who has never had the idea cross his mind of doing a detective story. Before Poe, there was none of this. He stands at the head of a genre, a profession, and an industry.

Although the craft has become more sophisticated in many ways, Poe scarcely seems old-fashioned in his methods. The "fair play" doctrine is, fully enunciated, a relatively recent addition to the rules of the game—the idea that the author must set out the clues in such a way as to give the reader as good a chance as the detective to solve the mystery. Entertaining stories have been written without regard to this rule, which is unknown in the best of two old masters, Wilkie Collins *(The Moonstone)* and Conan Doyle *(A Study in Scarlet).*

Poe obeyed the fair play doctrine in "The Purloined Letter," not deliberately but by a kind of instinct for what was fitting. The reader knows as much as Dupin and can, if mentally alert, reach the solution just as quickly. Poe puts the two necessary clues in their hands at the same time. The first clue is that the best way to hide an object is to leave it in the most obvious place. The second clue is that the missing object is a letter. If the reader joins the two clues as he should, he knows where the letter is.

Numerous *i*'s have been dotted and *t*'s crossed in the past century. Clues are scattered more artfully; criminals have become more cunning than they were; detectives in self-defense have become more acute. Criminals and detectives come from all the human types. Methods of murder include technical scientific discoveries from nuclear radiation to lethal microscopic organisms, and writers play with combinations of countless new factors available to them. A few of the later forms would have been beyond Poe. Not even he could have imagined the hard-boiled detective story of which Dashiell Hammett was the master —it is too much a product of twentieth century, post-World War I, America. Most of the other refinements would have been within Poe's range, and he might have introduced many of them if he had been writing detective novels. Being confined to the dimensions of the short story, he had to do what he could with the space at his disposal, where there was no possibility of trailing clues at twenty-page intervals. No one has used that amount of space more effectively. If Poe had written as much detective fiction as Conan Doyle, the world's most famous detective would be, not Sherlock Holmes, but C. Auguste Dupin.

The standards set by Poe are still sound. Today's practitioners are all in his debt. The Mystery Writers of America paid only part of the debt when they founded their Edgar Allan Poe Award for the best detective story of the year.

CHAPTER 5

Lyric Strains

THAT Poe contributed more to prose literature than to poetry was not a matter of personal choice with him. His profession and his hope of financial success made him set aside his verse against his will so that he might offer short stories for sale in the literary market place. His genius, ideally, would probably have held the balance equal between prose and poetry, and he would have turned out equal quantities of both. That they would have been equal in quality, too, is suggested by the high merit of the fifty-or-so poems that he managed to produce in spite of all obstacles.

He was a poet at heart. His first three volumes were of verse—*Tamerlane and Other Poems* (1827), *Al Aaraaf, Tamerlane, and Minor Poems* (1829), and *Poems* (1831). The last two volumes include reprints and revisions, and these are the first witnesses to his characteristic and lifelong habit of taking pains to improve his work from edition to edition.

As he began with poetry, he ended with it. His last year brought from him individual pieces as permanently popular as "For Annie" and "Annabel Lee." Between the beginning and the end he did not let his lyric inspiration die, but turned to poetry as often as he could. Four years before his death he published *The Raven and Other Poems* (1845). To this technical verse should be added prose like "The Colloquy of Monos and Una," which is very close to poetry. Poe's stories are sometimes similar to his poems in tone, mood and even events; and in some cases he introduces his poetry into his stories to add to the effect: "The Conqueror Worm" appears in "Ligeia"; "To One in Paradise" in "The Assignation"; and, the most powerful example, "The Haunted Palace" in "The Fall of the House of Usher."

Poe theorizes about poetry more than he does about prose. He repeatedly discusses verse and verse forms in his book reviews.

His "Poetic Principle," "Rationale of Verse" and "Philosophy of Composition" are elaborate essays wherein he sets forth his aesthetics of poetry at length.

I *The Meaning of Poetry*

The writer of so much *ad hoc* copy aimed at meeting deadlines could not avoid self-contradiction, much less the apparent inconsistencies that spring from the uses of language, especially from forgetfulness about how one has defined words in the past. That is one caveat. A second touches the question of intellectual development, and this is an acute problem in a discussion of Poe's poetry, because the longest career he enjoyed during his comparatively brief life was that of a poet. The youthful author of "Tamerlane" is not identical with the mature author of "Ulalume," nor can their attitudes toward poetry as an art be meshed without friction.

Still, there are contants throughout, and by identifying and interpreting these we may arrive at a systematic statement that Poe himself possibly would not have rejected, and that, should he have done so, might fairly be argued as something forced upon him by his own principles.

In his famous "Letter to B——," written as early as 1831, Poe offers a few hints about the attributes by which poetry may be recognized:

> A poem, in my opinion, is opposed to a work of science by having, for its *immediate* object, pleasure, not truth; to romance, by having for its object an *indefinite* instead of a *definite* pleasure, being a poem only so far as this object is attained: romance presenting perceptible images with definite, poetry with indefinite sensations, to which end music is an *essential,* since the comprehension of sweet sound is our most indefinite conception. Music, when combined with a pleasurable idea, is poetry; music without the idea is simply music; the idea without the music is prose from its very definitiveness.[1]

When Poe wrote this passage he was a young romantic poet, strongly influenced by Bryon, Moore and Shelley in his practice, just as strongly influenced by Schlegel, Shelley and Coleridge in his theory.[2] The passage starts him to theorizing about poetry, and is fundamental enough in his continuing thought to be used as a point of reference for what he says later on. It deserves, therefore, to be examined clause by clause.

The distinction between poetry and science ties in directly with his broad philosophy of aesthetics. Less than anywhere else in creative literature will he allow the "heresy of *The Didactic*" to contaminate poetry. The poem must neither teach nor preach, truth and goodness being pertinent only if they arise indirectly from the text. The poet must be a committed true believer in art for art's sake.

What is the object of poetry? The "Letter to B——" says that pleasure is the immediate object. "The Poetic Principle" says that beauty is the "province of the poem," and defines poetry as *"The Rhythmical Creation of Beauty."* The same work adds that "through the poem" the reader experiences a kind of divine joy.[3] The obvious inconsistencies of these *dicta* have caused Poe to be severely criticized for a confused thinker.[4]

But the inconsistencies are not so radical as they seem, for they come out of different contexts. If the effect on the reader is under discussion, then it is correct to say that pleasure is the object. Since this pleasure is caused by beauty, it is correct to say that beauty is the object. Since the poem is a construct in verse, it may properly be defined as the rhythmical creation of beauty. Since the elements out of which the poet makes his construct are not themselves created by him, the idea of creation has to be modified, therefore, by the thought that what the poet manufactures is the poem, and that what the poem does is to suggest an already existent beauty. The poem thus becomes a pipeline connecting the reader with the beautiful, and the beautiful is arrived at through, rather than in, the poem.

Poe follows the Platonic tradition. He agrees with Plato that there is a higher world of perfect Ideas, of which the world in which we live is but a copy. Things suggest Ideas; and beautiful things suggest the Idea of beauty. Between things and Ideas exists the world of art, the world that would not exist but for the work of the poet, the musician, the painter. The function of the poet, then, is to put words together in such a way as to give his reader a glimpse of Platonic beauty, and thereby to rouse in him the pleasure and the elevation of the soul that come from contact with the beautiful.[5]

Poe holds that the poet differs from the prose writer because he employs means that suggest indefinite, rather than definite, ideas and emotions. Both literary artists want to produce a desired effect. The story writer—whether his purpose is to amuse, to frighten, or to cause any other reaction—can pursue his aim with the unencumbered directness of Poe writing "The Cask of Amontillado." He can do this because he is working on manageable human reactions like humor and fear. He is in pursuit of a definite, unequivocal, emotional reaction; and he has a clear view of both his objective and the best way to reach it.

The poet, on the contrary, is trying to reveal an eternal beauty that he himself has never seen except in intermittent and oblique flashes. He cannot achieve his purpose except by capturing, as far as the resources of language permit, those intangible feelings that defy direct description. He must try to arouse the sense of beauty by indirection, by being suggestive and symbolical, by choosing his words so that their associations and sounds may carry overtones beyond their dictionary meanings.

This is one of Poe's essential ideas, and one of his most influential, for it hints at the later development of poetry into symbolism and impressionism. Especially in France, with Baudelaire and Mallarmé and Valéry, poetry entered into the domain of psychology that Poe had identified. All of these poets subordinated the direct statement in favor of a suggestiveness that ranged beyond the limits of direct speech. The handling of words became more subtle and refined as the search went on for new ways to perpetuate new experiences. Form began to dominate content as never before in the history of poetry.[6]

The theory is obviously not as all-embracing as Poe thought. It fits his own best poetry well enough, and the poetry of those inspired by him; but it does not cover the greatest poets of world literature. There is much more than Poe's concept of poetry in Homer, Dante, Shakespeare, and Goethe, all of whom are capable of doing what Poe says is impossible: expressing emotions like terror through genuine poetry. *King Lear,* to cite a clear case, bursts the bounds of poetry set by Poe. One of the most proper criticisms of Poe is that he is too addicted to identifying his personal art with universal art.[7]

Indefiniteness implies music. This is another basic proposition of Poe's artistic creed, for he believes that music is the most indefinite of the arts, and therefore that poetry can catch some of this quality by being infused with music. He makes this point in "The Poetic Principle."

It is in Music, perhaps, that the soul most nearly attains the great end for which, when inspired by the Poetic Sentiment, it struggles—the creation of supernal Beauty. It *may* be, indeed, that here this sublime end is, now and then, attained *in fact.* We are often made to feel, with a shivering delight, that from an earthly harp are stricken notes which *cannot* have been unfamiliar to the angels. And thus there can be little doubt that in the union of Poetry with Music in its popular sense, we shall find the widest field for the Poetic development.[8]

Poe puts the stages of poetry in the same ratio with music. Just as music finds its lowest level with program music (naturalistic music attempting to imitate the sounds of the world around us) and ascends by degrees to the highest level where it enters an artistic universe of pure form—just so does poetry rise from the definite imagery of the open eye to the indefinite impressions filtered "through the veil of the soul." Appropriately, several composers have been imspired by Poe to set his verses to music, and Ravel and Debussy have testified to his influence on their composition. "Edgar Allan Poe," wrote Debussy, "had the most original imagination in the world; he struck an entirely new note. I shall have to find its equivalent in music."[9]

Poetry differs from music by using ideas, and from prose by using music. Poe, naturally, does not mean that poetry presents clear ideas to be judged as true or false. He means that, for all his talk about indefiniteness and the flight of the imagination, poetry is knowledge. It is an insight into something objective—the eternal beauty that the poet wants to unveil as far as he can by means of his poetry. In Poe's review of Joseph Rodman Drake, he defines the love of poetry as "the sentiment of Intellectual Happiness here, and the Hope of a higher Intellectual Happiness hereafter." Poetry is one result of "the unconquerable desire—*to know.*"[10] From this thought sprang a more intellectualistic handling of poetry than romanticism had ever produced. The seeds of Neo-Realism are here.

Poe denies passion to the poet for the same reason that he denies it to any artist. *As a man,* of course, the poet must be passionate; he must perceive the existence of a Platonic world of ideal beauty; and he must feel ecstatic during his moments of enlightenment by it. *As an artist,* he must sit down to his work in the mood of a cool-headed craftsman able to think about the end he has in view and about the means that will take him most expeditiously to it. There is no contradiction in calling passion the enemy of poetry: It is the enemy of all art, once the artist has begun to put his vision into expressive form.

Poetry, again like all art, is partly intuition and partly hard work. This being so, Poe thinks that a poet should be able to explain the way his poem came into being. "The Philosphy of Composition" claims to do precisely that with "The Raven": Poe will take us into his workshop and show us how this one of his productions was conceived and executed. Whether or not Poe's memory was accurate, whether or not "The Raven" actually came into existence by the process he describes, "The Philosophy of Composition" reveals the way in which he considered a poem ought to be written.[11]

He begins by mounting one of his hobby horses—that of length. Just as he stands for brevity in prose, for the magazine story, he stands for brevity in poetry, for the poem that can be read in a single sitting. He calls the long poem a contradiction in terms since its object, the elevation of the soul, cannot be sustained for any degree of time. As might be expected, he argues also that unity fails. The epics of Homer and Milton he categorizes as successions of short poems divided by spaces that are prose but presented in poetic form.

His criterion is confused because he does not keep separate the poem as an objective thing and the psychological reaction of the reader. A long poem might be a true poem throughout, and the reader's interest might still flag through sheer weariness. Poe does not consider this possibility, or the possibility of a special aesthetic pleasure in coming back to a long poem over several sessions. As for unity, the *Iliad* has an architectonic unity with an aesthetic value of its own.

Poe says he began "The Raven" by deciding that he wanted about a hundred lines and that he ended with a hundred and eight. His objective is to elevate the souls of his readers by suggesting to them intimations of the perfect beauty that lies beyond this world. He here adds that the tone of the highest beauty in poetry is sadness and that melancholy, therefore, is "the most legitimate of all the poetical tones."[12]

This is another point of confusion. There would be no need to cavil at his principle that, since poetry reveals eternal joys that are now beyond us, there lies deep within it, therefore, the cause of sorrow. It has always been one of the fundamental aesthetic ideas that great art is closely connected with the tragic sense of life—Virgil's *lachrimae rerum,* "the tears of things." But this feeling is too profound a commentary on man's fate to be identified with melancholy in Poe's sense. It is only on a more superficial level that his theory can be sustained.

Poe's notion of the function of melancholy in poetry leads him to ask himself what is the most melancholy of subjects. "Death—was the obvious reply." He next asks when death is most poetical. "When it most closely allies itself to *Beauty:* The death, then, of a beautiful woman is, unquestionably, the most poetical topic in the world—and equally is it beyond doubt that the lips best suited for such a topic are those of a beareaved lover."[13]

This argument is so faulty that one may well feel that he ought to guard himself against the possiblity that "The Philosophy of Composition" is another of Poe's hoaxes. To reduce the notion of beauty to that of feminine beauty is almost bathetic; and it is obvious that the death of a *good* woman (Desdemona's tragedy) is at least as moving as the death of a *beautiful* woman. This brand of aesthetics has validity only for Poe and for those who think as he does.

He echoes in his theory the practice of his poems and stories. He has in mind his young, beautiful, doomed women like Annabel Lee, Eleanora and Madeline Usher. His remarks about the death of a beautiful woman must be seen against his related principle that the loftiest beauty always has something strange about it. The beauty he experiences certainly is infused with a strong dose of the strange, and he handles it with such consummate art that he would have been in an invulnerable position if he had restricted his theory to cover his own poetry and nothing more.

"The Philosophy of Composition" purports to show how Poe took the above ideas, added to them those he entertained about versification, and wrote "The Raven." That there are defects in his analysis has been shown. Again, he perhaps does himself an injustice in expounding so mechanical a process. He never touches intuition—imaginative insight—even though elsewhere he explicitly declares this to be a necessary part of poetry. The work is useful, however, for understanding Poe, once the exaggerations have been discarded and the confusions exposed; for, wherever his inspiration came from in the first place, it seems indubitable that as a craftsman he did work in some such fashion as that outlined in "The Philosophy of Composition."

The main lines of its theory of poetry can be checked against "The Poetic Principle" and against his reviews. The treatment of versification appears in lengthy exposition in "The Rationale of Verse." It is a pity that he wasted so much time on this essay, which, although it says much that is sound about poetizing, proves that he had no conception of the difference between English verse (based on accent) and Greek and Latin verse (based on syllabic length).[14] Fortunately his ear for the sounds of his own language was better than his "Rationale of Verse."

Poe wrote in "Marginalia" that genius is much more abundant than we think. He means that poetic inspiration is more widespread than the industry to exploit it; he means that potential poets are too lazy to make use of their gifts. He himself was not one of them. "The Philosophy of Composition" would be enough to tell us that if the rest of his works had vanished.

II *Symbols and Music*

Poe's poetry is less dependent than his prose on outside sources. So much is doubtless true of all writers who have worked in both fields, poetry being by its nature a much more *personal* thing than prose, catching nuances of temperament, feeling, and mood that escape the courser technique of expression. But with Poe the difference is wider than with most of the others. He could learn from his predecessors basic methods of achieving the effects of horror and terror, however much he might contribute from his personal experience and artistic genius. He could not learn in the same way how to present in verse his intuitive insights into Platonic beauty—his hypnagogic experiences on the threshold of sleep.

His poetry has little room for outside influences. True, he begins as a romantic poet who has avidly studied Bryon and Moore, imitating their subjects, styles, rhythms, lines; nor did he ever cease to read the poets of his time or to profit from his reading. The salient fact is that Poe quickly moves on from romanticism to new forms of poetry welling up from deep inside his own personality. He probes his subconscious by way of dreams and dreamlike states during which he hovered between sleep and wakefulness, ravished by beauties never present to him at any other time. Catching sight of strange visions and hearing strange harmonies, he is able to suggest them in words—and that is why he can write astounding poems the like of which had never before been known.

Poe's leap from romanticism to symbolism, impressionism, even surrealism, may be seen by comparing his first two long poems, "Tamerlane" and "Al Aaraaf." "Tamerlane" rings Byronically throughout. Its hero is one of the world's great conquerors, a chieftain of the marauding Mongol hordes—Tamerlane, whose armies spread death and devastation across Central Asia during the fourteenth century. The place, time, and character are colorful enough to satisfy the most demanding devotee of romanticism. The hero speaks in the romantic idiom of sated ambition, blighted love, and a determination not to submit to fate. There are great lines in "Tamerlane."

> I have not always been as now:
> The fever'd diadem on my brow
> I claim'd and won usurpingly—
> Hath not the same fierce heirdom given
> Rome to the Caesar—this to me?
> The heritage of a kingly mind,
> And a proud spirit which hath striven
> Triumphantly with human kind.

To read "Tamerlane" requires no more mental effort than to read Byron. "Al Aaraaf" is something entirely different: Poe moves onto a terrain, the various parts of which he will explore and map more carefully in subsequent poems. His imagination has begun to flower, his intuition to reach farther. The defect of "Al Aaraaf" is that the poet has not learned how to control his imaginative flights; he has not mastered the discipline of his craft, the laborious art of rethinking and refining and rewriting. He has broken through the limits of the romantic imagination without being able to exploit his breakthrough effectively. The poem is unorganized, confused, and in places seems close to meaningless.[15]

"Al Aaraaf" is the first example of Poe's mingling science with poetry. Taking the title from the Mohammedan name for limbo, a place in the hereafter where dwell neither the wholly good nor the wholly bad, Poe locates it on a star discovered by the Danish astronomer, Tycho Brahe, in the sixteenth century. This prosaic scientific reference would seem somewhat out of place in such a poem if we did not know of Poe's interest in the romance of astronomy. The science in "Al Aaraaf" is the more unusual because, in the same volume with it, Poe published a typical romantic protest against the havoc wrought in poetry by the discoveries of factual science. This is his admirable sonnet "To Science."

> Science! true daughter of Old Time thou art!
>   Who alterest all things with thy peering eyes.
> Why preyest though thus upon the poet's heart,
>   Vulture, whose wings are dull realities?
> How should he love thee? or how deem thee wise,
>   Who wouldst not leave him in his wandering
> To seek for treasure in the jewelled skies,
>   Albeit he soared with an undaunted wing?
> Hast thou not dragged Diana from her car,
>   And driven the Hamadryad from the wood
> To seek a shelter in some happier star?
>   Hast thou not torn the Naiad from her flood,
> The Elfin from the green grass, and from me
> The summer dream beneath the tamarind tree?

The author of this sonnet was on the surface a romantic poet ready to drink confusion to mathematics. "Al Aaraaf," refusing to persue the thought, recognizes the worth of astronomy even to the poet. From there Poe will go on to the prose poetry of "The Colloquy of Monos and Una" and "Eureka," and to his conclusion that the science of the stars is more poetic than anything the poet can imagine.

The locale of "Al Aaraaf" is a dream world full of ravishing sights, the spiritual home of the poet:

> Oh, nothing of the dross of ours—
> Yet all the beauty—all the flowers
> That list our Love, and deck our bowers—
> Adorn yon world afar, afar—
> The wandering star.

Al Aaraaf is a place where the Platonic Idea of absolute beauty can be known directly instead of through the imperfect things on the earth. Poe's poem is a hymn to the perfection that lies behind and explains the beautiful objects that we see around us:

> Now happiest, loveliest in yon lovely Earth
> When sprang the "Idea of Beauty" into birth
> (Falling in wreaths thro' many a startled star,
> Like woman's hair 'mid pearls, until, afar,
> It lit on hills Achaian, and there dwelt),
> She look'd into Infinity—and knelt.

The "She" mentioned here is one of Poe's strange ethereal women, in this case an astral goddess clothed in perfect beauty; but she nonetheless foreshadows the venerated mortal women with whom Poe will populate his later work. Nesace may live on a star, but something of her nature will reappear in Lenore and Annie. At one point "Al Aaraaf" becomes less cosmic by referring to the woman who will be the leading figure of one of Poe's best short stories:

> "Ligeia! wherever
> Thy image may be,
> No magic shall sever
> Thy music from thee."

Poe mourns his earth-bound existence—his exile from the Platonic universe of pure beauty—in "Israfel," where he again speaks of Mohammedan legend, this time of its heaven and of its lyrical angel. The poet would change places with the angel if only he could, for he feels hampered only by his human condition, not by his genius.

> If I could dwell
> Where Israfel
> Hath dwelt, and he where I,
> He might not sing so wildly well
> A mortal melody,
> While a bolder note than this might swell
> From my lyre within the sky.

When Poe repeated the dream-world theme in poems like "The City in the Sea," "The Valley of Unrest," and "Dream

Land,'' he made the uncanny more prominent; for he could use poetically as well as prosaically the dreams that are nightmares. The first stanza of ''Dream Land'' reads:

By a route obscure and lonely,
Haunted by ill angels only,
Where an Eidolon, named NIGHT,
On a black throne reigns upright,
I have reached these lands but newly
From an ultimate dim Thule—
From a wild weird clime that lieth, sublime,
Out of SPACE—out of TIME.

The note of melancholy, which is simply the fashionable romantic pessimisim in ''Tamerlane,'' becomes a cry of deep-seated, constitutional depression of the spirit in some of Poe's later works. ''The Haunted Palace'' is central to ''The Fall of the House of Usher'' because it parallels Roderick Usher's incipient madness. Poe laments the inevitable extinction that will surely engulf all of us in ''The Conqueror Worm,'' the meaning of which is summarized in the poem's concluding judgment of life,

That the play is the tragedy, ''Man,''
And its hero, the Conqueror Worm.

Poe's theory of poetry makes the death of a beautiful woman the most poetic of themes. His theory is undoubtedly defective; but he certainly acted on a sound instinct when he allowed it to guide his pen in writing ''Annabel Lee,'' ''The Raven,'' ''Lenore,'' and the other poems like them. It is almost mandatory to quote ''Annabel Lee'' at this point in a discussion of Poe's poetry.

It was many and many a year ago,
  In a kingdom by the sea,
That a maiden there lived whom you may know
  By the name of Annabel Lee;—
And this maiden she lived with no other thought
  Than to love and be loved by me.

A much better set of verses on the death of a beautiful woman is ''Lenore,'' the opening lines of which are superior to ''Annabel

Lee'' in every way:

> Ah, broken is the golden bowl—the spirit flown forever!
> Let the bell toll!—a saintly soul floats on the Stygian river:—
> And, Guy de Vere, has *thou* no tear?—weep now or nevermore!
> See! on yon drear and rigid bier low lies thy love, Lenore!

Poe's union of beauty and melancholy, not invented, but most forcefully stated and illustrated by him, was one reason for the practice of the decadent school of literature. Even Oscar Wilde reflected the influence of Poe when he wrote *Salome.*

The poem often considered to be Poe's best, his first ''To Helen,'' departs from his principle about joining beauty, love and death. ''To Helen'' is a love poem, one of the many he wrote for the women he knew. Its most familiar reference, however, has been taken out of context and used as the best comment ever made in two lines on the ancient civilization upon which the culture of the West is founded. Here is all of ''To Helen'':

> Helen, thy beauty is to me
> Like those Nicean barks of yore,
> That gently, o'er a perfumed sea,
> The weary, way-worn wanderer bore
> To his own native shore.
>
> On desperate seas long wont to roam,
> They hyacinth hair, thy classic face,
> Thy Naiad airs have brought me home
> To the glory that was Greece
> And the grandeur that was Rome.
>
> Lo! in yon brilliant window-niche
> How statue-like I see thee stand,
> The agate lamp within they hand!
> Ah, Psyche, from the regions which
> Are holy land!

This poem—with its low key, reasoned argument, controlled imagination, and classical restraint matching its classical allusion—was instrumental in the rise of neo-classical poetry. The French Parnassians made it their ideal to write just so.

As in his stories, Poe never let the melancholy or the uncanny monopolize his poems. "The Coliseum," again touching a classical subject, follows "To Helen." It is the poem that might have won a prize from the Baltimore *Saturday Visiter* except that the editors, having already awarded Poe their fiction prize for "MS. Found in a Bottle," decided that their poetry prize ought to go to someone else. Poe's pleasing sonnet "To My Mother" comes toward the end of his career, and so do the rhythmic triumphs, "The Bells" and "Eldorado."

The deeper element in Poe emerges in his symbolism which begins with "Al Aaraaf" and ends with "Ulalume." The first of these poems lays the ground for a universal poetry of symbols, allegories, and metaphors by postulating that

> All Nature speaks, and ev'n ideal things
> Flap shadowy sounds from visionary wings . . .

Symbolical connections, even when natural, are not necessarily easily identifiable. Where the symbols are artificial, the problem is much more complicated. This is the fundamental problem of all symbolism, the best of which is subtle and profound without losing its meaning. Poe objected to allegory and used it little because he thought it too obvious. His tendency is to work with symbols that are not allegories; and his vice is to be, not too obvious, but too abstract: The symbolism of "Al Aaraaf" is a subject of much dispute among Poe experts, and the poem will never be interpreted to everybody's satisfaction. Poe introduces symbols private to himself, so that in default of any explanation by the poet, the significance of the poem must remain dubious.[16]

When Poe came to the most celebrated of his poems, he chose to explain his method of operation. His "Philosophy of Composition" deals not only with the genisis of "The Raven" but also with the meaning of its symbols. The poem, of course, has a melancholy atmosphere which derives from what Poe's theory considers to be the most poetic of subjects—the death of a beautiful woman. Poe, who is fond of repeating feminine names, gives to this deceased woman the name Lenore. The poem turns on the questioning of the raven by the bereaved lover, and the answer to every question is "Nevermore." The climax of the poem comes when the raven responds with "Nevermore" to the question of whether the lover and his mistress may ever, in some future life, be reunited.

This meaning is on the surface. There is a second meaning that has to be interpreted through the symbols of the poem, through suggestive signs standing for ideas hidden below the surface. The raven is the principal symbol. By the common consent of mankind, the raven, with its jet black feathers and harsh croak, represents fate: It is, as Poe says, a "bird of ill omen," Therefore he found it pertinent to his poem. He then added a symbolical interpretation of his own. He tells us that *his* raven is "emblematical of *Mournful and Neverending Remebrance,"* which means that the bereaved lover, who is trying "to borrow/ From my books surcease of sorrow—sorrow for the lost Lenore," will now have his sorrow brought home to him in the most acute way by this creature that precisely stands for memory.[17] The symbolism reveals itself in the last stanza, which Poe wrote first since it is the culmination of the effect he wants to achieve:

> And the Raven, never flitting, still is sitting, *still*
> is sitting
> On the pallid bust of Pallas just above my
> chamber door;
> And his eyes have all the seeming of a demon's
> that is dreaming,
> And the lamp-light o'er him streaming throws
> his shadow on the floor;
> And my soul from out that shadow that lies
> floating on the floor
> Shall be lifted—nevermore!

The "bust of Pallas" is itself a symbol. Representing the Greek goddess of wisdom, it also represents the life of learning into which the narrator of the poem has plunged in order to drown his sorrow. At the same time, the sculpture contrasts with the raven perched on it—the one white and the other black, the one silent and the other croaking a single dismal word, the one symbolizing serene wisdom and the other crushing fate. The word "Nevermore" is also a symbol. As the poem progresses, the word sounds more and more like the booming of a gong; it begins to take on overtones of universal tragedy, reminding the reader that the tramp of death can be heard by us all, and not just by one individual asking about one dead woman.

The symbolism of "The Raven" is not difficult, and has not attracted the amount of critical commentary that surrounds "Ulalume," where Poe is suggestive in his most typical way. Even in his own time readers were baffled by "Ulalume," and he himself jokingly refused to explain the meaning. Poe scholars having performed this function for him, we know it signifies the impossibility of a new love replacing an old one. Words like "Auber" and "Weir" have been cleared up, although "Yaanek" remains bothersome, and "Ulalume" is only hesitatingly defined as "light in sorrow."[18]

But this poem did not have to await an *explication de texte* to be appreciated. It has been generally admired ever since it appeared. The reason is that it, like "The Raven" and so many other poems of the same weird type that Poe wrote, is infused with the music that no one but Poe could have put into words. At bottom it is his music that gives him a claim to the title of America's foremost poet. His ear for verbal sounds, verse forms, rhythm and rhyme permitted him to achieve the indefiniteness he wanted, to be suggestive where statement was impossible, to imply those vague fancies and half-dreams that escaped direct description. You do not have to be able to set down a coherent précis of "Ulalume" to be affected by such stanzas as:

> The skies they were ashen and sober;
>   The leaves they were crisped and sere—
>   The leaves they were withering and sere:
> It was night, in the lonesome October
>   Of my most immemorial year:
> It was hard by the dim lake of Auber,
>   In the misty mid region of Weir—
> It was down by the dank tarn of Auber,
>   In the ghoul-haunted woodland of Weir.

It is interesting to know just what a "most immemorial year" is, and why Poe selected the names "Auber" and "Weir." It is vital that the words *sound* exactly right in context, provoking in the reader a mood resonant with dim memories and hoary time and uncanny places; and that is why this poem produces the effect Poe was after even in those who have never bothered to look up the references in a critical edition.

"The Raven" is full of musical lines like these:

And the silken, sad, uncertain rustling of each
purple curtain . . .

. . . .

But the silence was unbroken, and the stillness
gave no token,
And the only word there spoken was the
whispered word "Lenore!"

. . . .

Then, methought, the air grew denser, perfumed
from an unseen censer,
Swung by seraphim whose foot-falls tinkled
on the tufted floor.

Poe's music moves even readers who point out that it is impossible for anything to tinkle on a tufted floor, let alone footfalls. The image does not have to be physically true to be set forth in beautiful verse.

Later poets have not been able to do much with Poe's music (although Vachel Lindsay echoes it). Many of them have done a great deal with his symbolism. One broad current of Western poetry is beholden to him, the current that runs, in Mattheissen's phrase, "from Poe through the symbolists to Eliot."[19]

As Poe's fiction has the vices of its virtues, so does his poetry. His poorer stories show up the tricks of his trade—the melodrama, the deliberate exaggerations, the stiff mechanical outer shell. His poorer poems do the same, for they expose in a cruel light the weakness that can betray the poet of melancholy, symbolism, and word music. In his first book of poetry he was capable of writing "Fairy Land," which opens thus:

Dim vales—and shadowy floods—
And cloudy-looking woods,
Whose forms we can't discover
For the tears that drip all over:
Huge moons there wax and wane—
Again—again—again—
Every moment of the night—
Forever changing places—
And they put out the star-light
With the breath from their pale faces.

Poe might be forgiven this youthful indiscretion were it not that he compounded the crime when he wrote "Eulalie" some fifteen years later. "Eulalie" begins well enough in Poe's customary vein: "I dwelt alone/ In a world of moan/ and my soul was a stagnant tide . . ." Poe then goes on to commit this artocity in his last stanza:

> Now Doubt— now Pain
> Come never again,
> For her soul gives me sigh for sigh,
> And all day long
> Shines bright and strong,
> Astarte within the sky,
> While ever to her dear Eulalie upturns her matron eye—
> While ever to her young Eulalie upturns her violet eye.

Even later, not long before his death, Poe began his second poem called "To Helen" in this fashion: "I saw thee once—once only—years ago:/ I must not say *how* many—but *not* many." It is useless to ask how the poet of the first "To Helen" could have written such stuff. Poe simply had Wordsworth's talent for writing heroically bad verse.

III *"The Jingle Man"*

Emerson once, while speaking with William Dean Howells, referred to Poe as "The Jingle Man."[20] The implication of the phrase is as clear as the dissimilarities that sundered Poe and Emerson, the poet from the seer, the artist from the metaphysician. Emerson was himself a poet, but one who used his verse as a vehicle for the truth, and who recoiled from Poe's doctrine of art for art's sake. Emerson could not see anything more than frivolity in Poe's experiments with sounds and verse forms; and he judged Poe to be a clever trifler, not a poet to be taken seriously—in short, "The Jingle Man."

The term "jingle" refers to the musical cantering of Poe's verse, a quality that is present in his best work, where the rhythm interpenetrates the sense in such a way that the two seem to go together naturally. To the examples given above we might add these.

> At midnight in the month of June,
> I stand beneath the mystic moon.
> —"The Sleeper"

Resignedly beneath the sky
The melancholy waters lie.
—"The City in the Sea"

I mourn not that the desolate
Are happier, sweet, than I,
But that *you* sorrow for *my* fate
Who am a passer by.
—"To ———"

Most critics would dissent from Emerson's opinion of such poetry, which has a powerful rhythmic quality even when it approaches a simple experiment in sound, when it pretends to suggest no ecstatic visions of the beautiful, when the ear becomes dominant and allows the mind to pause in its arduous quest for high significance. Nor need the defense of Poe rest its case at this point. He is never merely superficial. He is not a writer of light verse, but a poet; he is sometimes a bad poet, but the implication of the phrase "Jingle Man" is the reverse of the truth.

Two poems are distinctive in this respect: "The Bells," which is commonly slighted in an Emersonian fashion, and "Eldorado," which is commonly ignored. Both begin with a lilting beat that could hold them on the level of light verse, but both develop into something more profound. Both are jingles, if you like, but jingles with depth.

"Eldorado" was inspired, like "Von Kempelen and His Discovery," by the Gold Rush of '49. All America was aware of the hordes of men streaming toward California—toward the Sacramento and Sutter's Mill—all hopeful of striking it rich. The word "Eldorado" became a word as common in the American language as "sputnik" is today. It meant the far-off land of gold, sometimes with overtones of philosophical bliss; the latter is the sentiment Poe catches in his poem. As for crossing the continent to prospect for the precious metal, Poe banteringly denies his intention of doing so. To F. W. Thomas he wrote at this time:

Depend upon it after all, Thomas, literature is the most noble of professions. In fact, it is about the only one fit for a man. For my own part there is no seducing me from the path. I shall be a *litterateur,* at least, all my life; nor would I abandon the hopes which still lead me on for all the gold in California. Talking of gold and of the temptation at present held out to "poor-devil authors," did it ever occur to you that all that is really valuable to a man of letters —to a poet in especial—is absolutely unpurchasable? Love, fame, the dominion of intellect, the consciousness of power, the thrilling sense of beauty, the free air of Heaven, exercise of body and mind, with the physical and moral health which result—these and such as these are really all that a poet cares for:—then answer me this—*why* should he go to California?[21]

Poe takes up the impulse behind the Gold Rush, but gives to it a philosophical meaning, in "Eldorado."

Gaily bedight,
A gallant knight,
In sunshine and in shadow,
Had journeyed long,
Singing a song,
In search of Eldorado.

But he grew old—
This knight so bold—
And o'er his heart a shadow
Fell as he found
No spot of ground
That looked like Eldorado.

And, as his strength
Failed him at length,
He met a pilgrim shadow—
"Shadow," said he,
"Where can it be—
This land of Eldorado?"

"Over the Mountains
Of the Moon,
Down the Valley of the Shadow,
Ride, boldly ride,"
The shade replied,—
"If you seek for Eldorado!"

Of all Poe's poetry, the nearest thing to a pure jingle is "The

Bells." Here, where the appeal to the ear is immediate and inescapable, Poe achieves one of his most remarkable sucesses. World literature can scarcely show a more triumphant handling of onomatopeia—suggestiveness and meaning conveyed through the medium of sounds.

"The Bells" has always been a popular favorite from Poe, for he is at his most musical. He avoids monotony by cleverly varying the length and pattern of each stanza to fit the sequence of themes—sleigh bells, wedding bells, alarum bells, funeral bells —which build up into a crescendo of sound almost audible on the printed page. The first stanza starts the verse moving with the characteristic swing that pervades it to the end.

Hear the sledges with the bells—
Silver bells!
What a world of merriment their melody foretells!
How they tinkle, tinkle, tinkle,
In the icy air of night!
While the stars that oversprinkle
All the heavens, seem to twinkle
With a crystalline delight;
Keeping time, time, time,
In a sort of Runic rhyme,
To the tintinnabulation that so musically wells
From the bells, bells, bells, bells,
Bells, bells, bells—
From the jingling and the tinkling of the bells.

The sequence of themes prevents this poem from being light verse in the depreciatory sense. The bouncing melody becomes infused with a developing maturity of thought and feeling as it moves from the jolly sleigh bells and the happy wedding bells through the minatory alarum bells to the philosophical tolling of the funeral bells. The last stanza begins with the lines:

Hear the tolling of the bells—
Iron bells!
What a world of solemn thought their monody compels!
In the silence of the night,
How we shiver with affright
At the melancholy menace of their tone!

This is more than good light verse for declamation by the parlor elocutionist. It is poetry that affects the mind as well as the ear.

IV *"The Walloping Dactylic Metre"*

The most severe condemnation of Poe the poet by a prominent man of letters came from Aldous Huxley, who attributed to him a few virtues but numerous vices of the most stultifying kind.[22] Although Huxley acknowledges that "To Helen" and "The City in the Sea" are great poems, he considers the rest of Poe's poetry to be mainly a wasteland of bad taste, the effusions of a mind undeviatingly "vulgar" when it pretends to be lyrical.

Huxley begins his case against Poe in this vein: "Was Edgar Allan Poe a major poet? It would surely never occur to any English-speaking critic to say so."[23] This statement may be the most imprudent Huxley ever made because he allowed his ignorance to dictate to his judgment. Had he consulted the literature on the subject, he would have learned that Swinburne, Hardy, and Yeats, to mention only three of a host of English-speaking poets, all regarded Poe as a major poet.

Beginning his specific criticism, Huxley delcares: "The substance of Poe is refined; it is his form that is vulgar."[24] His test case is "Ulalume," of which "the walloping dactylic metre is all too musical."[25] His point is that the meter, which is supposed to support the poem, actually ruins it. Is this possible? Apparently not, by his own showing, for he remarks that Byron and Hood both used the dactylic form successfully. He attributes their success to their subject matter: They had the right substance to match the form. From this it follows that substance is the determining factor that makes or breaks a poem; that, if a poem is vulgar, the substance makes it so. But Huxley has termed Poe's substance "refined," which means that "Ulalume" is refined. Huxley is therefore entangled in illogicalities into which he has forced his argument.

To show his meaning in practice, he took the Proserpina theme from Milton and cast it into what he conceived to be the style of Poe:

It was noon in the fair field of Enna,
    When Proserpina gathering flowers—

Herself the most fragrant of flowers,
Was gathered away to Gehenna
By the Prince of Plutonian powers;
Was borne down the windings of Brenner
To the gloom of his amorous bowers—
Down the tortuous highway of Brenner
To the god's agapemonous bowers.

Having written this, Huxley says: "The parody is not too outrageous to be critically beside the point; and anyhow the music is genuine Poe."[26] This claim should be received with some reserve.

Huxley has not come within miles of "genuine Poe." The music of "Ulalume" does not lie simply in the dactylic form but derives from a blending of form and substance, of sound and sense. Huxley's flat parody catches none of Poe's unique effects. Huxley's feeble substance corrupts the form, and what he has proven is that dactylic meter alone does not make a poem musical. His parody *is* too outrageous, and it *is* critically beside the point. Successful parodies of Poe are always humorous; serious parodies are always unsuccessful. Huxley's failure stands as a warning against making the attempt to emulate Poe on his own ground.

CHAPTER 6

Critical Attitudes

THROUGHOUT Poe's practice of prose and poetry there runs a constant search for a correct theory of both, which means that he is by nature as much a critic as a writer. His philosophy of aesthetics presupposes a cultivated taste that reacts sensitively to great art. His standards of knowledge and craftsmanship impy an awareness of the elements and the structure that make art great. His taste and his awareness are constantly operating in his own work. He becomes a formal critic when he applies them to the work of other men.

He wrote more criticism than anything else. His editorial career would have forced him into book reviewing had he not loved it for its own sake, and hundreds of his reviews appeared in the magazines and newspapers with which he was connected. To these writings of the moment he added his major critical essays, the distillations of his principles in systematic form. He thus erected the third pillar that underprops his literary achievement. His criticism stands beside his short stories and his poems as a worthy contribution to America's literary heritage.

I *The Nature of Literary Criticism*

Poe, in preparing his book reviews and essays, drew on his predecessors at least as much as he did in his creative writings. Many of the guiding theories he follows had already been stated in books available to him; and their influence on his thought is indubitable despite his frequent failure, or refusal, to name them. Many ideas came to him indirectly, at second hand. Many ideas he simply took from the intellectual atmosphere around him. His claim to originality is less justified in his principles of criticism than in the actual opinions he passed on the authors he read.

The major thinkers behind his thought have already been

named. He looks for Platonic inspiration and Aristotelian unity. He sees Plato and Aristotle mainly through the eyes of Shelley and Schlegel. He is familiar with the British magazine discussions of Kames and Kant. His preferred master, to use a term that he would not have allowed, is Coleridge. If he did not read comprehensively or exhaustively in the giants of literary criticism, he read enough in them or about them to locate the concepts he needed.[1]

His vice is to trust too often to his secondary authorities to tell him what the primary authorities had said. This is notably true of his approach to Aristotle. As Poe trusts Mill to enlighten him about Aristotelian logic, so he trusts Coleridge to enlighten him about Aristotelian criticism; and when these two writers are wrong, Poe is wrong too. He states, following Coleridge, that Aristotle regarded poetry as the most philosophical of all literature.[2] Had he consulted the *Poetics* itself, he would have found Aristotle saying something quite different, namely that poetry is more philosophical than history. It is one more example of the misinformation and misinterpretation to which Aristotle has been subjected at every period since the Renaissance.

Poe gathers ideas from many sources. His personal contribution is to combine these ideas into a novel system, and then to apply the system to the judgment of individual writers.

Just as Poe believes in art for art's sake, so does he believe in criticism for criticism's sake. He recognizes that, while criticism would not exist at all except for pre-existing works of art, criticism has its own canons and laws which it may, and ought to, invoke without waiting for any other discipline. Poe gives the critic, too, a declaration of independence, proclaiming him to be under the authority of nothing but the standards of criticism. The critic is not a parasite who lives off other men for he has a unique function, the noble function of defending beauty and artistic representation. He has a duty to literature that no one else can perform: He must distinguish and isolate good writing from bad, pronouncing the former to be a legitimate occupant of the republic of letters, guiding the latter to oblivion that is its destination. To label a given work properly, and to give convincing reasons for so doing, is precisely the reason why Poe allows the critic a claim on our attention.

Criticism applies to itself as well as to creative literature. It is an important task of the critic to identify the canons of sound judgment and to decide whether critics in general, himself included, are handling the canons validly. Poe accepts this. He denies that one opinion is as good as another, or that there is any merit in the old tag: "There is no disputing about taste."[3] Disputing about taste was something he was always ready to do, and he never considered the dissenting opinions of other witnesses to be as acceptable as his own. This is not mere egotism; it is an assertion of the responsibility of the critic to know what he is talking about.

The point of departure in Poe's criticism is the thesis that "Every work of art should contain within itself all that is required for its own comprehension."[4] Extraneous facts, however interesting, are not relevant for Poe. He agrees that the critic may like to know, for example, the biography of the artist and the circumstances of composition, but he denies that such information should be allowed to affect critical opinion. It is *Hamlet* and not Shakespeare, *Faust* and not Geothe, that is being criticized. When Poe comes to *Barnaby Rudge,* he ignores Dickens the man, and focuses his critical apparatus squarely on the novel and nothing else.

He has a marked distaste for Macaulay's habit of confusing criticism with the historical essay. Macaulay's "review" of Ranke's *History of the Popes* "is nothing more than a beautifully written treatise on the main theme of Ranke himself, the whole matter of the treatise being deduced from the History. In the way of criticism, there is nothing worth the name."[5] What Poe missed in Macaulay was an analytical evaluation of Ranke's book.

Poe's attitude seems familiar to us of this generation. It is, in fact, the attitude of the New Critics of contemporary American literature, of those who have rebelled against sociological and other non-literary criteria, who have minimized the appeal to such things as psychoanalysis and economics, and who have placed little stock in the historical and background approach to literature. Critics like John Crowe Ransom, Allen Tate and R. P. Blackmur, in general, take the text to be self-sufficient for critical purposes.[6] By doing so, they hark back to their great forerunner. Poe was the first of the New Critics.

He refuses to let criticism take the easy way out. He refuses to let the critic lay aside aesthetic sensibility and intellectual rigor in favor of running down minute facts about an author's childhood, financial status, or motives for writing. He abhors the critic who talks around a text instead of sticking to it. He comprehends the reason why criticism so often becomes perverted in this way: Background research requires no particular ability, but criticism requires a distinct gift methodically applied.

Poe says that the critic of poetry must himself possess the poetic sentiment.[7] The idea is false if it refers to anything more esoteric than the human capacity to appreciate poetry (otherwise poets would be addressing one another rather than the public of non-poets); but it is noteworthy that the same kind of thought has been advanced by a modern poet and critic, T. S. Eliot, in his demand that his judges be made up of critics who are themselves poets.[8]

Poe's theory has another interesting clause. He holds that since poetry is knowledge, intuitive insight is more important than the specific poetic faculty, the faculty that fabricates the poem. Thus a man with no more than Dante's insight would come closer to writing true poetry than would a man with no more than Dante's genius at turning out *terza rima.* Here Poe submits to Shelley's analysis in *A Defence of Poetry,* the analysis ending with the conclusion that there has never been a greater poet than Plato, who did not write poetry as such, but who did enjoy ecstatic vision of the Platonic world of pure forms.[9] In other words, prose poetry is genuine poetry; intellectually impoverished rhyme is not.

Poe insists on the necessity for strong negative criticism: "He is to be hung? Then hang him by all means."[10] The sentiment is entirely consistent with Poe's character. Belligerent toward his opponents and contemptuous of work inferior to his own, he wields the scalpel of negative criticism with a loving hand. He will cheerfully expend pages on a mediocre poet like Joseph Rodman Drake to make sure that no flaw goes unmentioned. There is, at the same time, a perfectly sound and legitimate meaning in his opinion, for since the bulk of all published work is negligible, the critic is bound to look for the defects in any piece of writing offered to the public. Only thus can he force the worthless into the discard without waiting for time to do it, and only thus can he make the worthwhile shine splendidly by contrast.

When great literature has been discovered, then positive criticism identifies the merits that make it such. The poetic intellect of the critic perceives these merits. It fastens upon the beauties, the significant symmetries, the artistic cunning, the imaginative insight, of the writer. The critic's business is to make his perception public by explaining it in genuinely literary terms —in terms of unity over diffuseness, imagination over fancy, genius over talent, originality over imitativeness, pleasure over didacticism, meticulous craftsmanship over careless or slipshod scamping of the task.

Poe belongs to his time in his attack on literary nationalism, a cultural facet of the blatant Americanism that penetrated so deeply and so pervasively in the early nineteenth century. American writers were striving to be very American in their productions instead of following the old European models. There was much to be said for the movement as set forth by Emerson in *The American Scholar,* but with lesser men it degenerated and was expressed by the loud voice of extravagant patriotism.

Poe had a share in the nationalist extravaganza. He formed an alliance in New York with Evert Augustus Duyckinck and Cornelius Mathews, who were responsible for the Young America movement, which they promoted in their magazine *Arcturus.*[11] They and their followers called for a native tradition on this side of the Atlantic, and argued that material lay to hand on this continent that ought to form the subject matter of American literature. Poe did not write American literature in this sense; he took universal human themes, and his art could have been produced as easily had he been born in Europe; nevertheless, he deprecated the American habit of imitating past models and urged his fellow writers to become more independent.

Unlike most of Young America, he held the balance steady. He did not confuse patriotism with ability. He regarded nationalism as one of the most pestiferous of non-literary criteria, one of the worst of the corruptions of criticism that caused literature to deteriorate, and he continually scoffs at the strident patriots of letters. His review of Drake, a third-rate versifier widely acclaimed, makes the point that "so far from being ashamed of the many disgraceful literary failures to which our own inordinate vanities and misapplied patriotism have lately given birth, and so far from deeply lamenting that these daily puerilities are of home manufacture, we adhere pertinaciously to our original blindly conceived idea, and thus often find ourselves involved in the gross paradox of liking a stupid book the better, because, sure enough, its stupidity is American."[12]

Poe did not always live up to his prescription. He has a habit, when involved in controversies such as those surrounding Young America, of finding false beauties in the publications on his side, and false vices on the other side. But his faults do not harm his theory. He saw that a native tradition could not be sustained by lowering the critical standards for American authors. He makes Americans sit the literary test along with everybody else, and naturally most of them fail. The vulgar patriots could never understand that Poe thereby gave a new dignity to American letters.

II *"The Man with the Tomahawk"*

When in 1846 *Godey's Lady's Book* launched the series of critical articles by Edgar Allan Poe called "The Literati of New York City," the publisher, with a premonition of things to come, commented: "We are much mistaken if these papers of Mr. P. do not raise some commotion in the literary emporium."[13] Louis Godey could afford to make the observation with some detachment: He was not one of the literati. Those who *were* of the brotherhood felt differently about Poe's latest venture. Godey reported the fact the following month:

> We have received several letters from New York, anonymous, and from personal friends, requesting us to be careful what we allow Mr. Poe to say of the New York authors, many of whom are our personal friends. We reply to one and all that we have nothing to do but publish Mr. Poe's opinions, *not our own.* Whether we agree with Mr. Poe is another matter. We are not to be intimidated by a threat of the loss of friends, or turned from our purpose by honeyed words. Our course is onward.[14]

The literary atmosphere of New York, heated by the very thought of Poe's passing judgment on its lions of the moment, began to boil as his articles appeared and confirmed their fears. Soon the famous "War of the Literati" was on.

Poe already had a reputation as a critic, and his reputation was that of "The Man with the Tomahawk." For years he had been writing hostile, scathing, occasionally insulting, reviews of the journeymen of his trade; and he had not spared the illustrious. He had made a host of enemies. Those whom he did not like or admire knew in advance the kind of criticism to which they would be subjected, and that was the reason for the cries of alarm that greeted the *Godey's* announcement.

Poe did indeed use a "tomahawk" when he came to the negative part of his criticism, nor can the fact be explained by the simple assertion that he was doing his duty to the republic of letters by exposing inferior products. If some of his negative criticism adheres strictly to literary criteria, much of it reveals a personal bias that has nothing to do with poetic feet or with unity in the short story. Perhaps Poe deliberately started quarrels for the sake of publicity, or to increase the sales of the magazines he wrote for. The compelling motive, nonetheless, was his desire to strike at certain authors, and to strike at them as men, not merely as literary craftsmen.

All critics are subject to this vice. Personalities are necessarily involved in criticism, and one can find personal animus in the latest of the New Critics. For one with Poe's neurotic feelings, with his ability, failure, vanity, and tendency to identify criticism of himself with persecution, the tempation was extreme. No matter how strongly he may urge that the text is all-important for critical purposes, there are circumstances in which he simply cannot forget who the author is, and in which he cannot be dispassionate. Such are the cases when Poe mistakes, as Lowell said, "his phial of prussic-acid for his inkstand."[15] Such are the cases when he berates the critics whom he calls "Titmice" and "Tittle-bats."[16]

Since he resented Boston's cultural supremacy over the rest of the country, and especially over the South, and since he disliked the Transcendentalist movement, his references to the writers of New England are generally derogatory to the verge, if not beyond the verge, of contempt. Boston he customarily refers to as "Frogpondium," and the Transcendentalists are "Frogpondian Euphuists."[17] The *North American Review* he calls the *North American Quarterly Humdrum* in "Never Bet the Devil Your Head." To F. W. Thomas he wrote:

I wish you would come down on the Frogpondians. They are getting worse and worse, and pretend not to be aware that there *are* any literary people out of Boston. The worst and most disgusting part of the matter is that the Bostonians are really, as a race, far inferior in point of *anything beyond mere talent* to any other *set* upon the continent of

North America. They are decidedly the most servile imitators of the English it is possible to conceive. I always get into a passion when I think about it.[18]

For Emerson, the Transcendentalist who dismissed him as "The Jingle Man," Poe was bound to have an antipathy. The two men faced one another across their period, and have ever since, as the leaders of two opposed factions: Poe leading the poets who stand for art for art's sake, Emerson leading the prophets who cannot conceive of any significant writing independent of truth (as they understand it).

Poe's "Marginalia" makes Emerson "a respectful imitation of Carlyle," a comparison that should be checked against the assertion in the same writing that "The next work of Carlyle will be entitled 'Bow-Bow.' "[19] Poe, who used German idealism in "Eureka" and the cosmic romances, could not abide its less disciplined use by Carlyle, Emerson, and the Transcendentalists generally. For him, Emerson was a purveyor of mysticism for its own sake, the "Frogpondian Euphuist" par excellence, and a toplofty New Englander with a patronizing attitude toward writers from other regions of the country. Although much that Poe alleges against Emerson is perfectly justified, the asperity of the criticism is too sharp to come from textual analysis alone. Poe disliked Emerson as a man and thinker, and could not speak of him without becoming personal.

James Russell Lowell was another New England writer pilloried by Poe. Lowell admired the Boston literary scene and disliked slavery—two good reasons for Poe to attack him in print despite their amicable correspondence, their occasional expressions of mutual admiration, and Lowell's responsibility for Poe's invitation to speak in Boston at the time of the famous fiasco. In "Marginalia" Poe condemns Lowell for declaring that a writer can know theory without being able to reduce it to practice (a contradiction of one of Poe's basic tenents); and he declares him to be, with reference to one of the crazy figures of the French Revolution, "the Anacharsis Clootz of American letters."[20]

The act of Lowell that touched off Poe's temper more than anything else was the publication of *A Fable for Critics,* in which occur these lines about Poe:

> There comes Poe with his Raven, like Barnaby Rudge,
> Three-fifths of him genius and two-fifths sheer fudge,
> Who talks like a book of iambs and pentameters,
> In a way to make all men of common sense damn meters,
> Who has written some things quite the best of their kind,
> But the heart somehow seems all squeezed out by the mind.

Anyone else might have taken this passage as a compliment. Not many writers in world literature have been more than three-fifths genius. Poe being Poe, when *A Fable for Critics* arrived on his desk for review, he used the occasion for an attack on Lowell, who is pictured as an inferior poet, a ranting Abolitionist, a narrow-minded New Englander ("All whom he praises are Bostonians"), and a fool for letting his opponents put him in a passsion (this latter a vice from which Poe evidently regarded himself as free). Poe's summation on *A Fable for Critics* is that "no failure was ever more complete or more pitiable."[21]

Poe's aversion to New England was so strong that he even violated his principle about being gallant with the ladies: He both condemned critically and lampooned Margaret Fuller. His most cutting diatribe, however, he reserved for Henry Wadsworth Longfellow. It is not easy to understand what made Poe so angry with a writer who was not the type to cause or enter controversy. Longfellow's popularity may have been an irritation; so may the fact that he held a comfortable professorship at Harvard while Poe was scrabbling for a living in the competitive arena of the literary market place. In any case, Poe came to believe that Longfellow's shortcomings were being smothered in a fog of adulation by a Boston claque supporting a favorite son, and that he himself was doing American letters a favor by exposing the fact.

"The Longfellow War" may be followed through a sustantial part of one volume from Poe's collected works, and it is as unedifying as anything in which Poe ever engaged.[22] It belongs more to his biography than to his criticism, more to the facts of his life than to his judgment on authors. He is really speaking about Longfellow the man rather than Longfellow the poet. The whole episode looks the worse from Poe's side because in 1841, when he had asked Longfellow to contribute to *Graham's Magazine,* he had expressed "fervent admiration" for his work.[23] Poe himself felt hesitant about the request, and he could hardly have been surprised at Longfellow's begging off because of prior commitments. The year before, Poe had reviewed Longfellow's *Voices of the Night,* in the course of which review, while acknowledging merits in the poetry, he had accused the poet of plagiarism. Poe asserts that Longfellow's "Midnight Mass for the Dying Year" is an obvious steal from Tennyson's "The Death of the Old Year" (which is certainly false), and remarks with astounding savagery: "We have no idea of commenting, at any length, upon his plagiarism, which is too palpable to be mistaken, and which belongs to the most barbarous class of literary robbery: that class in which, while the words of the wronged author are avoided, his most intangible, and therefore his least defensible and least reclaimable property is purloined."[24]

That Poe should later go to Longfellow for contributions is not uncharacteristic. It belongs to that dichotomy of his personality, so evident in his dealings with John Allan, whereby he would first be insulting and then turn around and ask for help. Longfellow shows up better; for, never vindictive, a few months later he did publish poetry in *Graham's Magazine.*

In 1842, however, Poe returned to the attack when he reviewed Longfellow's *Ballads and Other Poems.* This time the critic remains more strictly critical. He had already accused Longfellow of most of the literary sins—no originality, no unity, no combining force, no steadily developing imaginative power. Now he focuses on one point—didacticism. This review has a long passage, repeated later in "The Poetic Principle," expounding art for art's sake and insisting that beauty and not truth is the end of poetry. Longfellow's sin, according to Poe, is that he makes truth rather than beauty the object.

What really infuriates Poe, however, is the thought of Longfellow as a plagiarist. Over and over again in subsequent publications he says that the Harvard poet is guilty of theft from other practitioners of the craft. Poe even complains that Longfellow passed off, as his own translation from the German, a ballad that already existed in English. The crowning injury, in Poe's view, was Longfellow's "borrowing" from "Politian" in writing "The Spanish Student."[25] It is doubtful that any of these charges of plagiarism can be sustained. Poe simply thought up accusations at a time when he felt that he must have them for some violent personal reason.

Poe had a long record of this kind of personal criticism when he sat down to write "The Literati of New York City: Some Honest Opinions at Random Respecting Their Authorial Merits, with Occasional Words of Personality." The bare title was sufficient to send a shudder through the literary circles of the city.

Actually, Poe did a favor, in the long run, even for those he ridiculed. He immortalized insignificant men and women who, except for their appearance in his gallery, would long since have disappeared from the history of American literature. But for Poe, who today would ever hear of George H. Colton, Laughton Osborn, William Kirkland, James Lawson, Elizabeth Bogart? Whether he praised or damned them, he rescued from oblivion over thirty New York personalities who were prominent in their own time and of no importance thereafter.

Although Poe often gave commendation where it was hardly due, he is best remembered for the negations implied in "The War of the Literati." He is venomous to a degree with those of the opposite faction, his "masterpieces" in this respect being his evaluations of Charles F. Briggs, Thomas Dunn English, and Lewis Gaylord Clark. Here are choice passages from his remarks about the three.

Now and then [Briggs] has attempted criticism, of which, as might be expected, he made a farce. The silliest thing of this kind ever penned, perhaps, was an elaborate attack of his on Thomas Babington Macaulay, published in "The Democratic Review"—the force of folly could no farther go. Mr. Briggs has never composed in his life three consecutive sentences of grammatical English. He is grossly uneducated.[26]

No spectacle can be more pitiable than that of a man [English] without the commonest school education busying himself in attempts to instruct mankind on topics of polite literature. The absurdity in such cases does not lie merely in the ignorance displayed by the would-be instructor, but in the transparency of the shifts by which he endeavors to keep this ignorance concealed.[27]

On account of the manner in which it is necessarily edited [Clark's *Knickerbocker Magazine*] the work is deficient in that absolutely indispensible element, *individuality,* as the editor has no precise characters, the magazine, as a matter of course, can have none. When I say "no precise character," I mean that Mr. C., as a literary man, has about him no determinateness, no distinctiveness, no saliency of point—an apple, in fact, or a pumpkin, has more angles. He is as smooth as oil or a sermon from Doctor Hawks; he is noticeable for nothing in the world except for the markedness by which is he noticeable for nothing.

Poe's "Literati" brought him numerous feuds in which he engaged with grim delight. His affair with Thomas Dunn English —whom he satirized as Thomas Done Brown—led to a court case after English accused Poe of forgery. Poe won legally, but the suit did not diminish his reputation for being "The Man with the Tomahawk."[29]

Admirers of Poe would like to draw a veil of charity over much of his derogatory criticism, if only they could. Abusing his undoubted genius for great literary analysis, he too often appears mean and petty. As his life reveals irrational deviations from his normal conduct, so does his criticism. Reviewing Hawthorne or Dickens, he can be as sane as any critic who ever lived. Dealing with his personal aversions, he declines from his own standards into something that can be called criticism only in a warped sense.

The final word should be left to the man whom Poe injured more angrily, and more irrationally, than anyone else. Longfellow delivered the noblest judgment ever passed by one American writer on another, when, after Poe's death, he wrote a letter praising Poe as both poet and prose master, and added of Poe the critic: "The harshness of his criticisms, I have never attributed to anything but the irritation of a sensitive nature, chafed by some indefinite sense of wrong."[30] Longfellow's judgment is charitable. It is also close to the truth.

III *The Just Judge*

When Poe laid aside his "tomahawk" (and he did so most of the time), he wrote as one of the masterly literary critics. The majority of his reviews are devoid of personal animus. Most are balanced and perspicacious; many throw off flashes of comprehension that come only from real genius; a few belong to the permanent classics of criticism. Poe's analysis of a text is often a model of how the thing ought to be done.

He could appreciate merits even in those he condemned. His review of Lowell's *Fable for Critics,* denunciatory as it is, defends both Lowell and Longfellow from Margaret Fuller's disparagement of them: "Messrs. Longfellow and Lowell, so pointedly picked out for abuse as the worst of our poets, are, upon the whole, perhaps, our best—although Bryant, and one or two others, are scarcely inferior."[31]

Poe is not just clearing the ground for a personal and neurotic attack on Lowell. He notes Lowell's proficiency in sentimental verse, and he is quite right in saying that Lowell's ear is defective when he writes satiric verse. As for Longfellow, Poe admits in the review of *Voices of the Night* that Longfellow is capable of occasional beauties and poetic insights, and he never goes back on that statement. If on one would want to "place" either Lowell or Longfellow in literary history simply on the basis of Poe's reviews, the reviews are not therefore irrelevant. They have to be accounted for in any definitive evaluation of these two American writers.

Poe's best criticism does not stand in need of similar qualifications. He is a just judge, sometimes the justest ever to pass a verdict on the writer in question. The forgotten poets J. G. C. Brainard and Thomas Ward never recovered, and never will recover, their reputations after Poe's handling of them. His criticism is derogatory—and just.

His best piece in this respect is his review of William Ellery Channing. He fastens on the essential point that Channing is a watered-down version of Tennyson, pushing to absurdity Tennyson's search for the quaint and the strange in poetry. Poe subjects Channing's verse to a technical examination and reveals the way in which he perverts the iambic meter by false accents, as in the line: "I leave thee, *the* maid spoke to *the* true youth." Poe ridicules Channing's solecisms ("infiniter," the comparative form of an adjective that has no comparative; the description of trees and girls as "sumptuous," meaning "costly"). In a few words Poe catches the nonsense in Channing's

I hear thy solemn anthem fall,
  Of richest song upon my ear,
That clothes thee in they golden pall
  As this wide sun flows on the mere.

Poe's criticism is: "Now let us translate this: He hears (Mr. Channing) a solemn anthem, of richest song, fall upon his ear, and this anthem clothes the individual who sings it in that individual's golden pall, in the same manner that, or at the time when, the wide sun flows on the mere—which is all very delightful, no doubt.''[32] No critic will ever save Channing from Poe's strictures, and probably none will ever want to.

Turning from the tearing down of false reputations to the building up of true ones, Poe is no less sound. He has many high achievements in positive criticism, the very highest being his reviews of Bryant, Hawthorne and Dickens.

In William Cullen Bryant, Poe found the poetic virtues he admired most—sense of beauty, creative imagination, musical ear, originality, form, techinique, laborious craftsmanship. Poe attaches to Bryant's verse epithets like ''especially beautiful'' and ''richly imaginative''; and, in a brief space, he produces enough evidence to support his judgment. He commends ''Thanatopsis'' and ''To a Waterfowl,'' then as now Bryant's most popular poems; but he gives his greatest praise to ''June,'' because, for one reason, it is so moving without being marred by passion (Poe, of course, holding that passion and poetry are inconsistent).

Poe, for whom the function of the poet is to elevate the soul, says that ''June'' does precisely that. He quotes the stanza beginning with the lines:

> And what if cheerful shouts at noon
>   Come, from the village sent,
> Or songs of maids, beneath the moon
>   With fairy laughter blent?

Poe's summation is: ''The thoughts here belong to the highest class of poetry, the imaginative-natural, and are of themselves sufficient to stamp their author a man of genius.''[33] Poe knew that Bryant's muse faltered from time to time, but he considered that his virtues so outweighed his vices that they made him an authentic poet of no mean stature.

Poe's most celebrated piece of literary criticism has Hawthorne for its subject. Here he sets down his philosophy of the short story. Here he gives good reasons for regarding Hawthorne as a master of the short story.

Reviewing *Twice-Told Tales* in 1847, Poe deplores the neglect of Hawthorne by the public and by those who should have known better—his colleagues of the reviews:

The daily critics would say on such occasions, "Is there not Irving, and Cooper, and Bryant, and Paulding, and—Smith?" or, "Have we not Halleck, and Dana, and Longfellow, and—Thompson?" or "Can we not point triumphantly to our own Sprague, Willis, Channing, Bancroft, Prescott, and—Jenkins?" but these unanswerable queries were never wound up by the name of Hawthorne.[34]

Poe's protest is a tribute to his critical faculties. He might have disparaged Hawthorne as a New Englander and an allegorist, since he detested both New England and allegory. Hawthorne, at the same time, had rebelled against the Transcendentalism of his region, and he possessed too much genius to be limited by a crude objectivication of subjective feelings and values. Poe, therefore was able to judge this particular writer without any particular bias.

Realizing that Hawthorne had learned from Tieck's Gothic romances, Poe realized also that Hawthorne had developed the form in a personal and inimitable way. *Twice-Told Tales* revealed to Poe the touch of a true master.

Of Mr. Hawthorne's *Tales* we would say, emphatically, that they belong to the highest region of Art—an Art subservient to genius of a very lofty order. We had supposed, with good reason for so supposing, that he had been thrust into his present position by one of the impudent cliques which beset our literature, and whose pretensions it is our full purpose to expose at the earliest opportunity; but we have been most agreeably mistaken. We know of few compositions which the critic can more honestly commend that these *Twice-Told Tales.* As Americans, we feel proud of the book.[35]

Poe discovered faults in Hawthorne, some real (too much allegory), some imaginary (plagiarism from "William Wilson" in "Howe's Masquerade"); he was by his very outlook on literature incapable of perceiving certain of Hawthorne's high virtues (the tragic sense of "Young Goodman Brown"); but he still formulated a good and objective "summary of Mr. Hawthorne's merits and demerits."

He is peculiar and not original—unless in those detailed fancies and detached thoughts which his want of general originality will deprive of the appreciation due to them, in preventing them from ever reaching the public eye. He is infinitely too fond of allegory, and can never hope for popularity so long as he persists in it. This he will not do, for allegory is at war with the whole tone of his nature. . . . He has the purest style, the finest taste, the most available scholarship, the most delicate humor, the most touching pathos, the most radiant imagination, the most consummate ingenuity. . . .[36]

The one real blunder in Poe's analysis is his remark about allegory. It is a pity that he did not live to read the allegorical novel Hawthorne published the year after Poe's death—*The Scarlet Letter*—in which Hawthorne reached the pinnacle of literature to which Poe's review of *Twice-Told Tales* pointed as his attainable goal if only he would stop allegorizing.

The long review that Poe devoted to *Barnaby Rudge* deserves special mention because it shows him at work in his critical laboratory, so to speak, examining an elaborate text to see whether it conformed to his specifications for good writing. It also shows him picking up the hint for his most famous poem.

Poe preferred the short story to the novel because the former permitted unity of effect to a degree that the latter could not match. Nevertheless, he was not incapable of recognizing the peculiar merits in a good novel (Defoe's craftsmanship in *Robinson Crusoe,* for example), and he finds much to praise in *Barnaby Rudge,* to which he was drawn in part because of the murder-and-mystery theme. He admired the extreme skill with which Dickens maintains the suspense, places clues, and leads on to a plausible solution. He takes the plot apart to prove that the author has generally played fair with the reader by stating falsehoods and misrepresentations, not in his own person as narrator, but through his characters. Poe obviously believed that he himself could have tightened up the plot by discarding what he considered irrelevancies (he thought the Gordon Riots out of place, although they are central for Dickens), but he still regarded the novel as a very good mystery story.

Poe's analysis of *Barnaby Rudge* can be supported by one remarkable piece of evidence. He first had occasion to mention the novel when it was running serially in its early installments; and he predicted, from the way the crime and the characters were depicted, that the murderer would prove to be Barnaby's father. Dickens is said to have been astonished by the feat.[37]

Among the defects of *Barnaby Rudge* Poe adduced the faulty presentation of the bird of ill-omen that struts through it.

The raven, too, immensely amusing as it is, might have been made, more than we see it, a portion of the conception of the fantastic Barnaby. Its croakings might have been *prophetically* heard in the course of the drama. Its character might have performed, in regard to that of the idiot, much the same part as does, in music, the accompaniment in respect to the air. Each might have been distinct. Each might have differed remarkably from the other. Yet between them there might have been wrought an analogical resemblance, and although each might have existed apart, they might have formed together a whole which would have been imperfect in the absence of the other.[38]

Poe himself undertook to correct Dickens' oversight. He composed "The Raven."

Poe's accomplishment in criticism does not, any more than in his stories and poems, mitigate his failures. He thought too much of Tennyson, too little of Burns. He minimizes the importance of Greek tragedy and belauds that minor fantasy, Foqué's *Undine.* He confessed to being profoundly moved by the death of Little Nell in *The Old Curiosity Shop,* a sentimental Dickensian scene of which Oscar Wilde declared that only a heart of stone could read it without laughing.

Either Poe's emotional nature or his character as a Southern gentleman, prompts him to be much too lenient with women writers. He can scarcely criticize a woman, however incompetent, without softening the blow by saying something complimentary. He gives the benefit of a very slim doubt to such nonentities as Amelia Welby, Elizabeth Oakes Smith, and Estelle Anna Lewis. He is too generous to Rufus Wilmot Griswold, who edited *The Female Poets of America* (and, as Poe's literary executor, betrayed him after his death).

Poe's failures, apart from his feuds and his friends, have two main causes. Sometimes he rides a hobby horse: he praises inferior works for their originality; he condemns superior works for lacking originality. Sometimes his judgments had to be formed too quickly because he lacked the time to do better. He was a hard-pressed reviewer writing to onrushing deadlines, and he had to deal with the latest books as they piled up on his desk in the publishing houses of the magazines for which he worked. No reviewer who ever labored in the field as seriously as Poe did has been exempt from prejudices or editorial pressures. Each has felt the sensation of drowning in a sea of books, and of none can it be claimed that he refused to cut corners or turn in less than his best copy when he felt time running out on him. What can be claimed for Poe is that, more than most, he kept his judgment in place and his head above water.

His critical virtues remain. His successes in judging books and authors are many and notable. As Edmund Wilson has said: "There is no other such critical survey in our literature."[39]

CHAPTER 7

The Permanence of Poe

THE literary criticism to which Edgar Allan Poe has been subjected is enough to create skepticism about literary criticism. The dogmatic assurance of fine critical minds when they disagree about Poe, the extremes of their disagreement, the fact that so many are drawn up on each side—all this might suggest that criticism is so subjective, so tied to whim and prejudice, as to render impossible any valid, objective judgment of Poe or of any other writer. Varieties of taste and differences of opinion are inevitable in the case of any author, but usually there is a broad area where a consensus may be said to exist—after negligible and incompetent critics stand on each side of the line confronting one Poe. Good critics stand on each side of the line confronting one another, and their confrontation creates a problem.

Quotations can be accumulated to prove that Poe is a second-rate hack or a creative genius who falls just short of the supreme masters. He is repeatedly called overrated, and underrated. In an amazing international clash of opinion, Americans marvel that Poe is highly esteemed in France, while Frenchmen marvel that Americans do not seem able to understand or appreciate the magisterial literary personality they have given to the world.

Two things are in dispute here: the writing that Poe himself did, and the writing he prompted other men to do. He can be examined either for his achievement or for his influence because the controversy in criticism concerns both.

I *Poe's Achievement*

The problem of Poe's achievement is summarized neatly in the contradictory opinions of two celebrated men of letters, both highly gifted practitioners of their art, both knowledgeable in the history of literature, both professional literary critics. Henry James remarks: "An enthusiasm for Poe is the mark of a decidedly primitive stage of reflection."[1] Edmund Wilson states: "Poe is not, as he is with the French and as he ought to be with us, a vital part of our intellectual equipment."[2]

Let it be said at once that Wilson is demonstrably right and James demonstrably wrong. To argue the reverse is to classify as "decidedly primitive" not only long-established masters like Baudelaire and Tennyson, but also such accomplished moderns as Valéry, Yeats, and Bernard Shaw. Complicating the issue, James appears later to have changed his mind about Poe, at least to the extent of developing an enthusiasm for (astonishingly) "Arthur Gordon Pym."[3]

But not all members of the anti-Poe chorus have sung different tunes at different times, and these are the ones who must be answered if a defense of Poe is to be made secure. Some derogatory pronouncements are sound enough to be accepted by those who admire him. He *is* sometimes too melodramatic, banal, subjective. The fallacy in this kind of criticism is that it can make any writer look foolish if judiciously applied to his shortcomings. If we jibe at the "tawdry tinsel" of Poe, we can just as easily jibe at the overblown pontifications of Emerson, at the turbid welter of Whitman, at the prissy perfectionism of James. Poe had his faults, but they are not, or ought not to be, the decisive factor in estimating him. He is too good too often to be so circumscribed.

He has the writer's primary virtue of readability, for he writes prose that moves vigorously and is almost never dull. His art is based on an ecomony of means, the ability to say in a few words what another writer would say in many. He is a master of the great line. He writes with power, producing in his finest works the effect that follows from an understanding of what to say and how best to say it. He is original in that he invented one type of literature, perfected others, and pointed the way in which still others ought to be pursued. He is versatile: poet, storyteller, critic; artist in humor and horror and beauty and fantasy; genius of the Gothic tale, and of satire on the Gothic tale; romanticist, realist, symbolist, surrealist; author of "To Helen," "The Black Cat," "The Poetic Principle," "Eureka," and the review of Hawthorne.

A man can enter many fields without justifiably claiming the ownership of any. This is not true of Poe. He has a strong claim to the titles of our best poet, our best short story writer, and our best critic. Whether each of these titles be genuine or not, the overall achievement they represent is not easily challenged by any other American author.

What, then, of the negative criticism? Some of it is simply false. No longer does anyone have to take Henry Seidel Canby seriously when he says that Poe lacked a sense of humor; or V.L. Parrington when he says that Poe had no interest in his America; or D.H. Lawrence when he says that Poe's work reveals the unstable emotional life of a dark necrophilist and opium addict.[4] The idea that Poe's principles of art and criticism are incoherent can be sustained only on the superficial level of passages lifted out of context. The old contemptuous opinion of Poe's cosmological fantasies is withering away as scholars probe more deeply into his theories of imaginative intuition in relation to scientific discovery.

Some of the negative criticism of Poe is simply a matter of personal preference. J.B. Priestley, unimpressed by "Ulalume," applies the epithet "faded theatrical backcloths" to such phrases as "dank tarn of Auber" and "ghoul-haunted woodland of Weir."[5] Since Priestley admits that "some good judges of literature" feel quite differently, he might have indicated that he was expressing nothing more than his own taste, from which anyone else is free to dissent. This kind of subjectivity is a common move in the game of denigrating Poe.

In general, it is possible to dislike the type of thing Poe did, even apart from the question of how well he did it. If critics do not like romanticism, surrealism, Gothic horror, detective stories, or verse that appeals primarily to the ear—they will not enjoy Poe. Every critic has his blind spots, and he has a right to them. He has no right, however, to make them the universal criteria of literature, and it is precisely the vice of doing so that makes so much criticism of Poe irrelevant.

T.S. Eliot has suggested that Poe's poetry ought to be viewed in the French fashion—in a body and not in isolated poems.[6] The same aesthetic logic is germane to the rest of Poe. He should be judged primarily, not as a poet or prose writer or critic, but as all three at once. Then his remarkable mastery of the field of letters becomes immediately apparent.

Poe has been damned as well as praised at every turn; but when wrangling over a writer's achievement has continued for so long and been sustained by critics so conflicting in their premises, it is safe to assume that his defenders are more nearly right than his disparagers. Negative criticism, the identification of defects is easy; and, if Poe has all the defects attributed to him, he should have been disposed of long ago. He has not been disposed of. His reputation, as resilient as he was, always bobs up after an attack, which suggests that he will never subside to the minor level to which the prosecution would like to see him sentenced.

Positive criticism, the identification of merits, is much more difficult; and yet in this respect Poe has been a beneficiary of recent thought. The Harvard edition of Poe, so notably begun by Thomas O. Mabbott, proclaims in its opening statement the theme for the whole work: "Edgar Allan Poe's position as a major author of poetry, fiction, and criticism is generally recognized. There has long been a need for a complete collection of his writings."[7]

Criticism now tends to ask, not whether Poe is a great writer, but why. His personality is seen in a much more balanced way than ever before because the more sensational allegations against him have been shown to be canards.[8] While no one denies his dark moods and neurotic compulsions, these are interpreted as limited to begin with and as sources of some of his best work.[9] That he was normal enough to read widely for usable sources, that he labored indefatigably at his editor's desk—facts as essential as these have been fully documented.[10]

Some of his works are more highly regarded than in the past. "Eureka" is attracting the attention it deserves.[11] "Arthur Gordon Pym" may not possess all the strange beauties and meanings that some critics have read into it, but it is being granted a more distinguished place in science fiction. The list of revised judgments favorable to Poe has grown longer partly because he was so much ahead of his own time and so much in tune with ours. We, for instance, can understand the alienated artist better than Poe's contemporaries could.

II *Poe's Influence*

At this point, half the case for Poe has been established, the half concerning his achievement. The other half concerns his influence. Some artists are great almost entirely through their achievement (Shakespeare, Mozart). Ohers are great not only because of their achievement but also because of their influence on their art (Beethoven, Cézanne). Still others have to their credit a body of great work, a controlling impact on their art, and a pervasive influence ramifying into other arts (Goethe, Scott). Poe belongs in the last category, and preeminently so.

In American literature, his influence affected writers from H.P. Lovecraft to Robert Frost; in English literature, writers from Tennyson to Graham Greene.[12] Foreign writers, certainly in all the major languages of the West and probably in most of those around the world, have submitted to Poe's influence.[13] The most noteworthy examples are Frenchmen.

The Franco-American relationship presents a unique puzzle. Long ago, when leading American critics were patronizing or contemptuous of Poe, French critics called him a classic and placed him beside Balzac, Dickens, and Tolstoy. This difference of opinion is so remarkable that one corner of Poe studies is devoted to possible explanations of Poe's influence in France.[14] The derogatory critics have usually taken the line that hostile Americans (and Britons) are better qualified than favorable Frenchmen to evaluate an American writer. These critics stress the argument that Baudelaire, Mallarmé, and Valéry must have been impressed by Poe because of their unfamiliarity with the English idiom, an unfamiliarity that made them praise faulty lines to which any English-speaking reader will, or at any rate should, take immediate exception.[15]

While this premise may be accepted, literally or for the sake of argument, the conclusion does not follow. Misjudgments of the variety indicated (even allowing the worst that can be said in this respect) do not imply an incomprehension of Poe. If the French writers, since they were reading in a language not their own, were wrong about various passages in Poe, no such argument applies to their understanding of what he was trying to do. Poetic feeling can be destroyed by a language barrier; ideas cannot. The French symbolists were frequently baffled by Poe's symbols, but they knew very well what they were about when they adopted his method of using symbols in poetry. They understood his endeavor to infuse poetry with music, and his experiments with verse forms. His art may have been opaque to them at times, but they were perfectly capable of grasping his notion that art is its own reward. They did not invent a mythical figure to whom to ascribe the origin of their type of literature;

they found him. They did not imagine a pre-existing foundation for their own literary structures; they discovered it. Otherwise, their adulation of their American predecessor would be the most incredible fantasy for which he was ever responsible.

What matters is not what French poets and short story writers *said* of Poe but what they *made* of him. And what they made of him was, among other things, one of the most respected schools of poetry, a school that T.S. Eliot has traced from Poe through the French poets to Yeats, Rilke, and himself.[16]

The significant truth is that France produced the writers who followed Poe into a new phase of modern literature before anyone else did. Americans came later. It is slightly preposterous to infer that there must have been something wrong with the French because from their ranks came the gifted disciples who could see where the master was pointing and act on his guidelines. There is something startling in the bland assurance of French ignorance—as if Poe's effect on Baudelaire were a curiosity of literary history.

Against the claim that Baudelaire never understood Poe's poetry is the claim that he improved upon Poe's prose. Poe's stories are thus greater in the French translation than in the original—Baudelaire transmuted Poe into something better than he is. This assertion should never be allowed to go by. Baudelaire did indeed make certain improvements, by tightening lines, for example, and by choosing more precise words; but he did so only where Poe was not in complete control of his art. To the best of Poe, the criticism does not apply, for the best of Poe is very nearly beyond improvement. Baudelaire did not improve "The Cask of Amontillado" because Poe left him no chance to do so. The uncanny power of "The Fall of the House of Usher" belongs to Poe, not to Baudelaire.[17]

If Poe had influenced only Baudelaire, there might be some point in scoffing at Baudelaire's opinion. If Poe had influenced French poets only, there might be some point (although it would be as intangible as a Euclidean point) in scoffing at French opinion. Poe's influence, on the contrary, as been felt in prose and criticism as well as in poetry; and it has been felt throughout the Western world, including the English-speaking world where no problem of a language barrier could arise.

Poe's literary achievement, great as it is, does not surpass his influence. No other of his fellow countrymen, in any field, subject, discipline, or department of thought, has been so masterly in producing fruitful ideas for other men to cultivate. None has been so perceptive in so multifarious a way of the paths to the future that writers might tread. Even his personal prose was effective. It helped to form the attitude of the typical romantic poet, and it pointed forward to Oscar Wilde the aesthete, to Rossetti the Pre-Raphaelite, to Whistler and his fierce defense of "art for art's sake."

We are not yet finished with Poe's influence, which extends far beyond literature. His imprint is on art and music, on the type of painting and design associated with Aubrey Beardsley, on the musical scores of Debussy, Ravel, and Prokofiev.

The Debussy reference is particularly important because it shows Poe influencing in a major way a major figure from an entirely different field than his own.[18] After Debussy became interested in Poe early in his career through his reading of Baudelaire's translation, he confessed himself "haunted" by the weird characters and uncanny atmosphere of the Gothic tales. Not unexpectedly, he preferred "The Fall of the House of Usher" to all the rest. In 1910 he was working on a symphonic treatment of "Usher" using "psychologically developed themes."[19] This composition, which was never finished, is now lost.

In 1893 Debussy began work on *Pelléas et Mélisande,* an opera doubly Poesque in that both composer and librettist (Maeterlinck) took their inspiration from Poe. At this time Debussy wrote that Poe, "although dead, exercises over me an almost agonizing tyranny. I forget human feelings and shut myself up like a beast in the House of Usher."[20] His musical imagination kept struggling with the problems of transferring Poe's ideas from literature to music, but he had not yet solved all the problems when *Pelléas* appeared in 1903.

Poe became a direct and consuming interest for Debussy in 1908 when he agreed to do something from the Poe canon for the Metropolitan Opera in New York. He began to fashion two short operas from the tales: "Usher," for its Gothic terror; "The Devil in the Belfry," for its irony. This time Debussy was his own librettist. He wrote the entire libretto for "Usher," part of the "Devil" libretto, and fragments of the music for both. We know that he scored the cataclysmic final scene of "Usher" for drums, gongs, and cymbals, and that he would have used the gigue rhythm for "Devil" so that he could reflect in music the awkward, grotesque movements of the character.[21]

Debussy was not simply drawing on Poe's literature for stories in the way that Boito used Shakespeare for Verdi. He was writing Poesque music. He was writing operas in which words and music would be unified in a single Poesque entity. Enough is known of what he would have accomplished for a musicologist to say: *"Pelléas, The Fall of the House of Usher, Wozzeck, Il Prigionero, The Turn of the Screw*—the line of the aesthetic development of twentieth century opera is clear."[22]

Poe's comprehensive influence ought now to be pursued and documented in a survey covering at least Europe and America. This project would be one of the most worthwhile that any scholar could undertake. It would also be one of the most exacting, for the author would have to range from Canada to Russia, from Argentina to Scandinavia; he would have to branch from literature into art, music, and science; and he would have to explain how submission to Poe's theory or practice, or both, unites such strange allies as the symbolists and the naturalists, the decadents and the new critics, Maeterlinck and Conan Doyle, Jules Verne and Whistler, Swinburne and Dostoevski.

A survey of this type would leave, not Poe's reputation, but wonderment at it, looking meretricious. Poe would be revealed for what he is—America's greatest writer, and the American writer of greatest significance in world literature.

Notes and References

Chapter One

1. F.O. Matthiessen quotes Whitman approvingly in *American Renaissance* (New York, 1941), p. 541. Many books that approach Poe from the same point of view indicate the fact by their very titles: Jacques Bolle, *La Poésie du cauchemar* (Neuchatel, 1946); Marie Bonaparte, *Edgar Poe, étude psychoanalytique* (Paris, 1933); Nicolas-Isadore Boussoulas, *La peur et l'univers dans l'oeuvre d'Edgar Poe; une métaphysique de la peur* (Paris, 1952); Emile Lavrière, *Le génie morbide d'Edgar Poe* (Paris, 1935); John Robertson, *Edgar A. Poe: a Psychopathic Study* (New York, 1923); Frances Winwar, *The Haunted Palace: a Life of Edgar Allan Poe.* Many other books do not give a forewarning in their titles even though their content is similar to these. Two of the most noteworthy are D. H. Lawrence, *Studies in Classical American Literature* (London, 1924); Joseph Wood Krutch, *Edgar Allan Poe: a Study in Genius* (New York, 1926).

2. N. Bryllion Fagin, *The Histrionic Mr. Poe* (Baltimore, 1949); James S. Wilson, "The Devil Was In It," *American Mercury,* XXIV (1931), 215-20; Walter Fuller Taylor, "Israfel in Motley," *Sewanee Review,* XLII (1934), 330-40; Clark Griffith, "Poe's 'Ligeia' and the English Romantics," *University of Toronto Quarterly,* XXIV (1954), 8-25.

3. Camille Mauclair, *Le génie d'Edgar Poe* (Paris, 1925). Among the American critics who feel that there is more to be said for Mauclair's side of the argument than for the other are Margaret Alterton and Hardin Craig, introduction to *Edgar Allan Poe: Representative Selections* (American Book Company, 1935); T. O. Mabbott, introduction to *Selected Poetry and Prose of Edgar Allan Poe* (New York, 1951); Jay B. Hubbell, *The South in American Literature* (Durham, N.C., 1954), pp. 528-50; F. O. Matthiessen, "Poe," *Sewanee Review,* LIV (1946), 175-205.

Chapter Two

1. *The Complete Works of Edgar Allan Poe,* ed. James Harrison (New York, 1902), XVI, 165-66. Hereafter referred to as *Works.*

2. *Ibid.,* 312.

3. *Ibid.* I, 345. This imaginative "autobiographical" note is more important for Poe's attitude to himself than for the facts about him. He

never shared Byron's wanderlust, much less Byron's quixotic willingness to sacrifice himself for an ideal.

4. Edith Birkhead, *The Tale of Terror* (London, 1921), pp. 185-220; Palmer Cobb, *The Influence of E.T.A. Hoffmann on the Tales of Edgar Allan Poe* (Chapel Hill, N.C., 1908); Gustave Gruener, "Notes on the Influence of E.T.A. Hoffmann upon Edgar Allan Poe," *Publications of the Modern Language Association,* XIX (1904), 1-25.

5. Margaret Alterton, *Origins of Poe's Critical Theory* (Iowa City, 1925), pp. 7-45.

6. *The Letters of Edgar Allan Poe,* ed. John Ward Ostrom (Cambridge, Mass., 1948), pp. 57-58. Hereafter referred to as *Letters.*

7. *Works,* I, 151.

8. I have treated this subject more extensively in "A Note on Poe and Mesmerism," *The Wizard from Vienna: Franz Anton Mesmer* (New York, 1975), pp. 219-26. See also S.E. Lind, "Poe and Mesmerism," *Publications of the Modern Language Association,* LXII (1947), 1077-94; Doris V. Falk, "Poe and the Power of Animal Magnetism," *ibid.,* LXXXIV (1969), 536-46. Hervey Allen has a few pages on American occultism of the period, *Israfel: The Life and Times of Edgar Allan Poe* (New York, 1934), pp. 537-39.

9. The literature on romanticism as an idealogy is immense. For a good sketch of its attitudes, see Bertrand Russell, *A History of Western Philosophy* (New York, 1945), pp. 675-84. Russell says elsewhere, putting the thing in a nutshell, that "the romantics were in favour of living dangerously," *Wisdom of the West* (New York, 1959), p. 232. For specific references to Poe within the romantic movement, see Mario Praz, *The Romantic Agony,* tr. Angus Davidson (London, 1933), *passim;* C.M. Bowra, *The Romantic Imagination* (Cambridge, Mass., 1949), pp. 174-96.

10. *Works,* XVI, 88-89.

11. *Ibid.,* X, 30.

12. *Ibid.,* XVI, 164. Poe's experiments with sensory perception deserve more study than they have received for their bearing on the relationship between psychology and the arts.

13. *Ibid.,* 183. See also Floyd Stovall, "Poe's Debt to Coleridge," *University of Texas Studies in English,* X (1930), 70-127.

14. *Works,* XVI, 167. Carathis is the witch in William Beckford's Gothic novel, *Vathek.*

15. *Letters,* p. 73.

16. *Works,* I, 182.

17. Poe's scathing comment is given in full in Arthur Hobson Quinn, *Edgar Allan Poe: A Critical Biography* (New York, 1941), pp. 485-88.

18. Hervey Allen, in presenting this extraordinary scene (pp. 444-47), comments: "Mr. Poe, as usual, wore a Spanish-looking cloak and it was his peccadillo while in Washington to insist upon wearing it

wrongside out, an eccentricity that certainly did cause somewhat of a sensation . . . ."

19. *Ibid.,* p. 21.
20. *Letters,* p. 78.
21. The Poe-Allan quarrel has been discussed in many books and at great length, for example, by Hervey Allen and Arthur Hobson Quinn. No one doubts that there is something to be said on both sides. Perhaps the most balanced verdict is by Edmond Jaloux (basically anti-Allan), *Edgar Poe et les femmes* (Geneva, 1942), pp. 57-58.
22. Allen, p. 310.
23. Poe's relations with women will probably never be satisfactorily explained. Jaloux has devoted a book to the subject, a moderate treatment that ought to be read as an antidote to the psychoanalysts.
24. On the whole subject of Poe's marriage, see Quinn, *passim;* Jaloux, pp. 149-69.
25. *Letters,* p. 356.

Chapter Three

1. *Letters,* p. 57.
2. Allen, pp. 194-95.
3. *Letters,* p. 41.
4. Allen, p. 525.
5. For Poe's feeling about money and about his debts, see Quinn, p. 95. Bayard Taylor's parody in Poe's verse form on Poe's debt to Horace Greeley is in Edmund Wilson, *The Shock of Recognition* (New York, 1943), pp. 311-12.
6. *Works,* XVI, 169. Allen Tate remarks that Poe was a religious man who could not find a satisfying Christianity among the creeds he knew: "The Angelic Imagination: Poe and the Power of Words," *Kenyon Review,* XIV (1952), 455-75.
7. Allen, p. 308. Poe's stature as a humorist has become undeniable since the publication of the following works: Constance Rourke, *American Humor* (New York, 1931), pp. 145-49; C. Alphonso Smith, *Edgar Allan Poe: How to Know Him* (Indianapolis, 1921), pp. 50-56; Walter F. Taylor, "Israfel in Motley," *Sewanee Review,* XLII (1934), 330-40; James Wilson, "The Devil Was In It," *American Mercury,* XXIV (1931), 215-20; Napier Wilt, "Poe's Attitude toward His Tales," *Modern Philology,* XXV (1927), 101-5; Clark Griffith, "Poe's 'Ligeia' and the English Romantics," *University of Toronto Quarterly,* XXIV (1954), 8-25.
8. *Works,* XVI, 168.
9. A major trend of Poe scholarship at the moment stresses his interest in social and political problems. See Henry W. Wells, *The American Way of Poetry* (New York, 1943), pp. 19, 27-28; Haldeen

Braddy, *Glorious Incense: the Fulfillment of Edgar Allan Poe* (Washington, 1953), p. 62; Herbert M. McLuhan, "Edgar Poe's Tradition," *Sewanee Review,* LII (1944), 24-33; William Whipple, "Poe's Political Satire," *University of Texas Studies in English* XXXV (1935), 81-95; Ernest Marchand, "Poe as Social Critic," *American Literature,* VI (1934), 28-43. Among the older critics, Smith, pp. 26-37, had anticipated this new emphasis.

10. Poe broke with Lowell, for one reason because of Lowell's Abolition sentiment. See *Letters,* pp. 427-28.

11. *American Renaissance,* pp. 201-2. Van Wyck Brooks makes the same point in *The World of Washington Irving* (New York, 1944), pp. 25-26.

12. *Letters,* pp. 401-2. That Poe was an habitual opium addict is argued by Allen, pp. 641-42, but for a specific and convincing refutation, see Jaloux, pp. 123-32.

13. *Works,* XVI, 6-7.

14. *Ibid.,* XIV, 272-73.

15. Vincent Buranelli, "Pascal's Principles of Philosophy," *The New Scholasticism,* XXX (1956), 330-49.

16. Coleridge's distinction of the faculties is classical: *Biographia Literaria,* ch. XIII. Basil Willey discusses this part of Coleridge in *Nineteenth Century Studies* (New York, 1949), pp. 10-27.

17. John Stuart Mill, *A System of Logic,* II, I, 185-87. Mill uses the term "ratiocination" as a synonym for deduction. A critique of Poe's logic is Denis Marion, "La méthode intellectuelle de Poe," *Mesures,* VI (1940), 89-172.

18. *Works,* XVI, 192.

19. *Ibid.*

20. *Posterior Analytics,* 100. There are good discussions of this passage in Sir David Ross, *Aristotle,* 4th ed. (London, 1949), p. 39; H. W. B. Joseph, *A Modern Introduction to Logic,* 2nd ed. (Oxford, 1916), p. 391.

21. *Letters,* p. 380.

22. *Works,* XVI, 197. The philosophy of "Eureka" has been attracting attention ever since Paul Valéry wrote his enthusiastic appraisal "Au sujet d'Eureka," *Variétiés* (Paris, 1923), pp. 113-36. Each of the following works contributes something to an understanding of that philosphy: Frederick Drew Bond, "Poe as Evolutionist," *Popular Science Monthly,* LXXI (1907), 267-74; George Norstedt, "Poe and Einstein," *Open Court,* XLIV (1930), 173-80; Philip P. Wiener, "Poe's Logic and Metaphysic," *The Personalist,* XIV (1933), 268-74; Clayton Hoagland, "The Universe of Eureka," *Southern Literary Messenger,* new series, I (1939), 307-13; L. J. Lafleur, "Edgar Allan Poe as Philosopher," *The Personalist,* XXII (1941), 401-5; Frederick W. Conner, "Poe's Eureka: the Problem of Mechanism," *Cosmic Optimism*

(University of Florida, 1949), pp. 67-91; Clarence R. Wylie, Jr., "Mathematical Allusions in Poe," *The Scientific Monthly,* LXIII (1946), 227-35; Edward H. Davidson, *Poe: a Critical Study* (Cambridge, Mass., 1957), pp. 223-53.

23. *Works,* XIV, 133-49.
24. *Ibid.,* XVI, 206, and *passim.*
25. *Ibid.,* 26.
26. *Ibid.,* I, 275.
27. See Alterton, pp. 132-83, for research into Poe's sources.
28. *Letters,* pp. 381-82.
29. *Ibid.,* p. 260.
30. The strongest arguments for Poe as a harbinger of later science are by Norstedt and Hoagland.
31. The Eddington and Bauer letters are in, respectively, Quinn, pp. 555-56, and Bonaparte, pp. 619-21.
32. *Du cheminement de la pensée* (Paris, 1931), III, pp. 938-39.
33. *Works,* VIII, 294-95.
34. Albert J. Lubell, "Poe and A. W. Schlegel," *Journal of English And Germanic Philology,* LII (1953), 1-12; James Southall Wilson, "Poe's Philosophy of Composition," *North American Review,* CCXXIII (1926), 675-84; George Kelly, "Poe's Theory of Beauty," *American Literature,* XXVII (1956), 521-36.
35. *Works,* XIV, 275-76.
36. *Ibid.,* 271.
37. *Ibid.,* 272.
38. *Ibid.,* 271-72.
39. See Emerson's essay "The Poet" and Ralph L. Rusk, *The Life of Ralph Waldo Emerson* (New York, 1949), p. 301.
40. *Works,* XVI, 156.
41. *Ibid.,* 28.
42. *Ibid.,* 57.
43. *Ibid.,* 164.
44. *Ibid.,* 292.
45. *Ibid.,*
46. *Ibid.,* 69.
47. Allen Tate, "The Angelic Imagination," p. 469.
48. *Ibid.,* pp. 457-58.
49. *Ibid.,* p. 457.
50. Tate makes this point with regard to a greater writer than Poe: "It was not Ugolino, it was Dante who wrote about Ugolino with more knowledge than Ugolino had." See "Our Cousin, Mr. Poe," *Partisan Review,* XVI, 1218.

Chapter Four

1. *Works,* XVI, 118.

2. *Ibid.*
3. *Ibid.*, XIV, 74.
4. *Ibid.*, XI, 108. See F. L. Pattee, *The Development of the American Short Story* (New York, 1923), pp. 115-44.
5. *Works,* XI, 122.
6. *Ibid.*, XVI, 67.
7. *Ibid.*, XIV, 73.
8. Quinn, P. 745.
9. *Works,* III, xxxvii-ix. The problems surrounding this projected volume are discussed by T. O. Mabbott, "On Poe's 'Tales of the Folio Club,' " *Sewanee Review,* XXXVI (1928), 171-76.
10. Patrick F. Quinn, *The French Face of Edgar Poe* (Southern Illinois Press, 1957), pp. 169-215; Davidson, pp. 156-80.
11. Bonaparte, pp. 312-13 and 312-27, *passim;* Leslie A. Fiedler, *Love and Death in the American Novel* (New York, 1960), pp. 370-82.
12. Allen, p. 379.
13. Alterton and Craig, cxv-cxviii.
14. *Letters,* p. 309.
15. This argument would be beside the mark if "Ligeia," in spite of what seems its evident meaning, could be considered either the subjective nightmare of a disordered brain, Roy P. Basler, "The Interpretation of 'Ligeia,' " *College English,* V (1944), 363-72; or another Poe burlesque of the Gothic horror story, Clark Griffith, "Poe's 'Ligeia' and the English Romantics," *University of Toronto Quarterly,* XXIV (1954), 8-25.
16. *Letters,* pp. 57-58.
17. *Works,* X, 37.
18. Good discussions of this great short story are in Darrel Abel, "A Key to the House of Usher," *University of Toronto Quarterly,* XVIII (1949), 176-85; Leo Spitzer, "A Reinterpretation of 'The Fall of the House of Usher,' " *Comparative Literature,* IV (1952), 351-63; Maurice Beebe, "The Fall of the House of Pyncheon," *Nineteenth Century Fiction,* XI (1956), 1-17; Charles Feidelson, *Symbolism in American Literature* (Chicago, 1953), p. 35; Davidson, pp. 196-98.
19. C. P. Cambiare, *The Influence of Edgar Allan Poe in France* (New York, 1927), pp. 257-63; Régis Messac, *Le 'Detective Novel' et l'influence de la pensee scientifique* (Paris, 1929), pp. 305-80.
20. *Works,* XI, 109.
21. Mozelle S. Allen, "Poe's Debt to Voltaire," *University of Texas Studies in English,* XV (1925), 63-75.

Chapter Five

1. Alterton and Craig, p. 248.
2. Killis Campbell, *The Poems of Edgar Allan Poe* (Boston, 1917), pp. xliv-liii. Hereafter referred to as *Poems.* See also James Routh,

"Notes on the Sources of Poe's Poetry: Coleridge, Keats, Shelley," *Modern Language Notes,* XXIX (1914), 72-75; Floyd Stovall, "Poe's Debt to Coleridge," *University of Texas Studies in English,* X (1930), 70-127; H. T. Baker, "Coleridge's Influence on Poe's Poetry," *Modern Language Notes,* XXV (1910), 94-95.

3. *Works,* XIV, 275.

4. Yvor Winters, "Edgar Allan Poe: a Crisis in the History of American Obscurantism," *American Literature,* VIII (1937), 319-40; Charles C. Walcutt, "The Logic of Poe," *College English,* II (1941), 438-44; Joseph Chiari, *Symbolisme from Poe to Malarmé* (London, 1956), pp. 92-116. Convincing replies to this kind of criticism may be found in Marvin Laser, "The Growth and Structure of Poe's Concept of Beauty," *Journal of English Literary History,* XV (1948), 69-84; George Kelly, "Poe's Theory of Beauty," *American Literature,* XXVII (1956), 521-36.

5. Poe got his Platonism mainly by way of Shelley. See Norman Foerster, *American Criticism: a Study of Literary Theory from Poe to the Present Day* (New York, 1928), p. 32.

6. Louis Seylaz, *Edgar Poe et les premiers symbolistes français* (Lausanne, 1923), pp. 175-78.

7. W. C. Brownell, *American Prose Masters: Cooper—Hawthorne—Emerson—Poe—Lowell—Henry James* (New York, 1909), p. 247.

8. *Works,* XIV, 274-75.

9. May Garrettson Evans, *Music and Edgar Allan Poe: a Bibliographical Study* (Baltimore, 1939). The Debussy quotation is on the title page. The same subject is treated by Charmenz S. Lenhart, *Musical Influence on American Poetry* (Athens, Ga., 1956), pp. 125-60.

10. *Works,* VIII, 283.

11. Quinn, p. 440.

12. *Works,* XIV, 198.

13. *Ibid.,* 201.

14. Quinn, p. 561; W. L. Werner, "Poe's Theories and Practice in Poetic Technique," *American Literature,* II (1930), 157-65.

15. *Poems,* pp. 171-73.

16. Floyd Stovall, "An Interpretation of Poe's 'Al Aaraaf,' " *University of Texas Studies in English,* IX (1929), 106-33; Richard Wilbur, *Poe, Laurel Poetry Series* (New York, 1959), pp. 124-31; Alterton and Craig, pp. 479-90; Davidson, 13-31. C. M. Bowra analyzes the symbolist movement in European literature, and refers to Poe in the background, in *The Heritage of Symbolism* (London, 1943).

17. *Works,* XIV, 208. From the growing literature about this poem, the following may be cited as especially useful: Howard Mumford Jones, "Poe, 'The Raven,' and the Anonymous Young Man," *Western Humanities Review,* IX (1955), 127-38; Henry W. Wells, *The American Way of Poetry* (New York, 1943), p. 22; Alterton and Craig, pp. 500-4;

Davidson, pp. 76-104; Wilbur, pp. 142-45; *Poems,* pp. 246-56.

18 The best analysis of the poem is by Thomas O. Mabbott, *Explicator,* I (1942), 25, VI (1948), 57, and selections, p. 412. James Miller, Jr., defends it from its detractors, " 'Ulalume' Resurrected," *Philological Quarterly,* XXXIV (1955), 197-205.

19. *American Renaissance,* p. 10.

20. Van Wyck Brooks, *Howells: His Life and World* (New York, 1959), p. 19.

21. *Letters,* pp. 426-27.

22. Aldous Huxley, "Vulgarity in Literature," *Music at Night and Other Essays* (New York, 1930), pp. 243-303.

23. *Ibid.,* p. 267.

24. *Ibid.,* p. 268.

25. *Ibid.,* p. 270.

26. *Ibid.,* p. 272.

Chapter Six

1. John Paul Pritchard, *Criticism in America* (Norman, Okla., 1956), pp. 70-86; Albert J. Lubbell, "Poe and A. W. Schlegel," *Journal of English and Germanic Philology,* LII (1953), 1-12; Alterton, *passim.*

2. Alterton and Craig, p. 243.

3. Pritchard, p. 78.

4. *Works,* XIII, 86.

5. *Ibid.,* X, 158.

6. Pritchard, pp. 231-65.

7. *Works,* XVI, 101.

8. For a logical refutation of the argument, with Eliot as the text, see C. S. Lewis, *A Preface to Paradise Lost* (Oxford, 1942), pp. 9-11.

9. *Works,* XVI, 101.

10. *Works,* XVI, 12.

11. Perry Miller, *The Raven and the Whale* (New York, 1956), pp. 88, 112.

12. *Works,* VIII, 277. "Exordium," Poe's important credo on the relation of nationalism to criticism, is in XI, 1-8.

13. *Ibid.,* XV, viii.

14. *Ibid.*

15. Quinn, p. 432.

16. *Works,* XI, 39-40.

17. *Ibid.,* XVI, 172. See also "Boston and the Bostonians," XIII, 1-13.

18. *Letters,* p. 427.

19. *Works,* XVI, 122, 175.

20. *Ibid.,* 70.

21. Lowell's *Fable for Critics* and Poe's reaction to it are in Edmund Wilson, *op. cit.*

22. *Works,* XII, 41-106.
23. Quinn, pp. 316-17.
24. *Works,* XI, 85.
25. Quinn, p. 454, estimates the justice (or injustice) of Poe's charges against Longfellow.
26. *Works,* XV, 22.
27. *Ibid.,* 65.
28. *Ibid.,* 115.
29. On this whole subject, see Sidney P. Moss, "Poe and His Nemesis—Lewis Gaylord Clark," *American Literature,* XXVIII (1956), 30-49; Francis B. Demond, "The War of the Literati," *Notes and Queries,* CXCVIII (1953), 303-8; Miller, *passim.*
30. Quinn, p. 655.
31. *Works,* XIII, 170.
32. *Ibid.,* XI, 184.
33. *Ibid.,* XIII, 135.
34. *Ibid.,* 142-43.
35. *Ibid.,* XI, 110.
36. *Ibid.,* XIII, 145.
37. Allen, p. 410; Brooks, p. 344. But the story is questioned by Gerald G. Grubb, "The Personal and Literary Relationship of Dickens and Poe," *Nineteenth Century Fiction,* V (1950), 11-12.
38. *Works,* XI, 63.
39. *The Shock of Recognition,* p. 80. Laudatory judgments on Poe as critic are also in George Saintsbury, *A History of Criticism and Taste in Europe* (London, 1904), pp. 634-36; Summerfield Baldwin, "The Aesthetic Theory of Edgar Poe," *Sewanee Review,* XXVII (1918), 210-21.

Chapter Seven

1. Henry James, *French Poets and Novelists* (London, 1878), p. 76.
2. Edmund Wilson, *The Shock of Recognition,* p. 84.
3. In Henry James' *The Golden Bowl,* Prince Amerigo is evidently speaking for the author.
4. Henry Seidel Canby, *Classic Americans* (New York, 1931), pp. 271, 276, 307; V.L. Parrington, *Main Currents in American Thought* (New York, 1927), II, 57; D.H. Lawrence, *passim.*
5. J.B. Priestley, *Literature and Western Man* (New York, 1960), p. 157.
6. T.S. Eliot, "From Poe to Valéry," *Hudson Review,* II (1949), 327-42.
7. *Collected Works of Edgar Allan Poe. Volume I. Poems* (Cambridge, Mass., 1969), preface, p. xvii.
8. Edward Wagenknecht, *Edgar Allan Poe: the Man Behind the*

Legend (New York, 1963), p. 13; Geoffrey Rans, *Edgar Allan Poe* (London, 1965), pp. 101-10; Floyd Stovall, *Edgar Poe the Poet: Essays Old and New on the Man and His Work* (Charlottesville, Va., 1969), pp. 181-86; Roger Forclaz, *Le Monde d'Edgar Poe* (Berne, Suisse, 1974), *passim.*

9. Harry Levin, *The Power of Blackness: Hawthorne, Poe, Melville* (New York, 1958), pp. 104-05; G.R. Thompson, *Poe's Fiction: Romantic Irony in the Gothic Tales* (Madison, Wis., 1973), pp. 5-8.

10. Burton R. Pollin, *Discoveries in Poe* (Notre Dame, Ind., 1970); Robert D. Jacobs, *Poe, Journalist and Critic* (Baton Rouge, La., 1969).

11. Richard P. Benton, *Poe as Literary Cosmologer. Studies on 'Eureka': a Symposium* (Hartford, Conn., 1975).

12. Wagenknecht, pp. 6-7.

13. William T. Bandy, *The Influence and Reputation of Edgar Allan Poe in Europe* (Baltimore, 1962). On specific languages, the following publications are of note: Carl L. Anderson, *Poe in Northlight: the Scandinavian Response to His Life and Work* (Durham, N.C., 1973); Joan Delaney Grossman, *Edgar Allan Poe in Russia: a Study in Legend and Literary Influence* (Würzburg, 1973).

14. The basic consideration of the French problem is Patrick F. Quinn, *The French Face of Edgar Poe* (Southern Illinois, 1957) supplemented by his *Poe and France: the Last Twenty Years* (Baltimore, 1970).

15. Marcus Cunliffe, *The Literature of the United States* (London, 1954), pp. 66, 71-72; Priestley, p. 217; Huxley, pp. 267-68.

16. T.S. Eliot, *Notes Towards the Definition of Culture* (New York, 1949), p. 115. The English-speaking reader may follow this current of poetry in Haldeen Braddy and Patrick F. Quinn, and pinpoint it by individuals in *Baudelaure on Poe: Critical Papers,* tr. Lois and Francis Hyslop, Jr., (State College, Pa., 1952); Enid Starkie, *Baudelaire* (London, n.d.), pp. 213-24; Stéphane Mallermé, *Selected Prose, Poems, Essays, and Letters,* tr. Bradford Cook (Baltimore, 1956); Norman Suckling, *Paul Valéry and the Civilised Mind* (London, 1954), pp. 58-95.

17. Roger Asselineau challenged my opinion of Poe-Baudelaire in his review of my book, Etudes Anglaises, xviiie année (1965), 96-97. My reply "Some Observations on Poe" and his rejoinder "A propos de quelques observations sur Poe" are on pp. 404-05. For a defense of Poe, see Claude Richard's review of Yves Florenne's edition of Baudelaire in *Poe Studies,* I (1968), 11-12, and his important review article, "Poe Studies in Europe: France," *ibid.,* II (1969), 20-23.

18. Edward Lockspeiser, *Debussy et Edgar Poe* (Monaco, 1961), and "Debussy and Edgar Allan Poe," *The Listener,* LXVIII (1962), 609-10.

19. Lockspeiser, *Debussy et Edgar Poe,* p. 47.

20. *Ibid.,* p. 48.

21. The text of Debussy's "The Fall of the House of Usher" is printed, *ibid.*, pp; 85-97; it is followed by music he is known to have composed for the two Poe operas.

22. Lockspeiser, "Debussy and Edgar Allan Poe," p. 610.

Selected Bibliography

This list of authors and publications is, despite the additions, proportionately smaller than in the first edition. Since interest in Poe has undergone a rejuvenation, much more is being written about him than ever before; but, by the same token, we have better tools for the retrieval of information and the collation of data, which means that a volume such as this can cover much of the ground by referring the reader to them. The most important tool that did not exist fifteen years ago is *Poe Studies,* a communal effort in the pages of which the latest scholarship and criticism may be followed. After this basic periodical come the comprehensive Poe bibliographies and indexes published in the past few years. These publications do not, of course, absolve a writer on Poe from the obligation to name what he considers the more important recent contributions. To keep the list within manageable limits, I have confined the additions mainly to books, allowing in only a few entries from the mass of articles, lectures, and notes. To avoid padding, I have left out of the bibliography some items mentioned briefly in the notes and references.

PRIMARY SOURCES

Collected Works of Edgar Allan Poe. Ed. by Thomas O. Mabbott *et al.* Cambridge, Mass.: Harvard University Press, 1969 -. The first volume, *Poems,* has been published.

The Complete Works of Edgar Allan Poe. Ed. by James A. Harrison. New York: Thomas Y. Crowell, 1902.

The Complete Poems and Stories of Edgar Allan Poe with Selections from His Critical Writings. Ed. by Arthur Hobson Quinn and Edward H. O'Neill. New York: Knopf, 1946.

Edgar Allan Poe: Representative Selections. Ed. by Margaret Alterton and Hardin Craig. New York: American Book Company, 1935.

Selected Poetry and Prose of Edgar Allan Poe. Ed. by Thomas O. Mabbott. New York: Random House, 1951.

Edgar Allan Poe: Selected Prose and Poetry. Ed. by W. H. Auden. New York; Holt, Rinehart and Winston, 1950.

Great Short Works of Edgar Allan Poe. Ed. by G. R. Thompson. New York: Harper and Row, 1970.

Introduction to Poe: a Thematic Reader. Ed. by Eric W. Carlson. Glenview, Ill.: Scott, Foresman, 1967.

Politian: an Unfinished Tragedy. Ed. by Thomas O. Mabbott. Richmond, Va.: Edgar Allan Poe Shrine, 1923.

Eureka: a Prose Poem by Edgar Allan Poe. New Edition with Line Numbers, Exploratory Essay, and Bibliographical Guide. Ed. by Richard P. Benton. Hartford, Conn.: Transcendental Books, 1974.

The Poems of Edgar Allan Poe. Ed. by Killis Campbell. Boston: Ginn, 1917.

Poe: Complete Poems. Ed. by Richard Wilbur. New York: Dell, 1959.

The Complete Poetry and Selected Criticism of Edgar Allan Poe. Ed. by Allen Tate. New York: New American Library, 1968.

Literary Criticism of Edgar Allan Poe. Ed. by Robert L. Hough. Lincoln, Neb.: University of Nebraska Press, 1965.

The Letters of Edgar Allan Poe. Ed by John Ward Ostrom. New York: Gordian Press, 1966.

SECONDARY SOURCES

1. Bibliographies

DAMERON, J. LASLEY and IRBY B. CAUTHEN, JR. *Edgar Allan Poe: a Bibliography of Criticism, 1827 - 1967.* Charlottesville, Va.: University of Virginia Press, 1974.

EVANS, MAY GARRETSON. *Music and Edgar Allan Poe: a Bibliographical Study.* Baltimore: Johns Hopkins Press, 1939.

HUBBELL, JAY B. "Poe." In *Eight American Authors: a Review of Research and Criticism.* Ed. by Floyd Stovall. New York: Norton, 1971.

HYNEMAN, ESTHER F. *Edgar Allan Poe: Annotated Bibliography of Books and Articles in English, 1827 - 1973.* Boston: G. K. Hall, 1974.

LUDWIG, RICHARD M. "Edgar Allan Poe." In *Literary History of the United States.* Ed. by Spiller, Thorpe, Johnson, and Canby. New York: Macmillan, 1948. Volume III, 689-96; *Bibliography Supplement,* ibid., 1959, 178-80; *Bibliography Supplement II,* ibid., 1972, 237-39.

2. Indexes

BOOTH, BRADFORD A. and CLAUDE JONES. *A Concordance of the Poetical Works of Edgar Allan Poe.* Baltimore: Johns Hopkins Press, 1941.

DAMERON, J. LASLEY and LOUIS C. STAGG. *An Index to Poe's Critical Vocabulary.* Hartford, Conn.: Transcendental Books, 1966.

GALE, ROBERT. *Plots and Characters in the Fiction of Edgar Allan Poe.* Hamden, Conn.: Archon Books, 1970.

POLLIN, BURTON R. *Dictionary of Names and Titles in Poe's Collected Works.* New York: Da Capo, 1968.

———. *Poe, Creator of Words.* Baltimore: Enoch Pratt Free Library, 1974.

ROBBINS, J. ALBERT. *Checklist of Edgar Allan Poe.* Columbus, Ohio: Ohio State University Press, 1969.

ROGERS, DAVID. *The Major Poems and Tales of Edgar Allan Poe.* New York: Monarch Press, 1965.

3. Authorities

ABEL, DARREL. "A Key to the House of Usher." *University of Toronto Quarterly,* XVIII (1949), 176-85. An interpretation of the story as a psychological allegory, the technique of which anticipates that of Kafka.

ALLEN, HERVEY. *Israfel: the Life and Times of Edgar Allan Poe.* New York: Farrar and Rinehart, 1934. Biography by a famous novelist that is more important for sympathetic understanding than for factual accuracy.

ALLEN, MICHAEL. *Poe and the British Magazine Tradition.* London: Oxford University Press, 1969. Monograph about Poe's use of popular writing to produce a higher type of literature.

ALLEN, MOZELLE S. "Poe's Debt to Voltaire." *University of Texas Studies in English,* XV (1935), 63-75. An investigation of how far Dupin resembles Zadig.

ALTERTON, MARGARET. *Origins of Poe's Critical Theory.* Iowa City: University of Iowa, 1925. An exhaustive research into Poe's reading and his adaptation of what he read.

ANDERSON, CARL L. *Poe in Northlight: the Scandinavian Response to His Life and Work.* Durham, N.C.: Duke University Press, 1973. Survey of Poe's influence in the Nordic nations.

ASSELINEAU, ROGER. *Edgar Allan Poe.* Minneapolis: University of Minnesota Press, 1970. A belated reappearance of the vulgar, horrific Poe.

BALDWIN, SUMMERFIELD. "The Aesthetic Theory of Edgar Poe." *Sewanee Review,* XXVII (1918), 210-21. Essay that makes Poe a forerunner of modern criticism in the arts.

BANDY, W.T. *The Influence and Reputation of Edgar Allan Poe in Europe.* Baltimore: Cimino, 1962. A quick look at the transatlantic acceptance of Poe.

———. "New Light on Baudelaire and Poe." *Yale French Studies,* X (1953), 65-69. A note showing that Baudelaire's early Poe criticism was affected by his knowledge of American sources.

BASLER, ROY P. "The Interpretation of 'Ligeia.' " *College English,* V (1944), 363-72. The interpretation is that this story is about abnormal psychology, not the supernatural.

BAUDELAIRE, CHARLES. *Baudelaire on Poe: Critical Papers.* Translated by Lois and Francis E. Hyslop, Jr. State College, Pa.: Bald Eagle Press, 1952. Reflections on Poe by the greatest of his disciples.

BEEBE, MAURICE. "The Fall of the House of Pyncheon." *Nineteenth Century Fiction,* XI (1956), 1-17. An interesting parallel study of celebrated works by Poe and Hawthorne.

BELDEN, HENRY M. "Observation and Imagination in Coleridge and Poe: a Contrast." In *Papers, Essays, and Stories by His Former Students in Honor of the Ninetieth Birthday of Charles Frederick Johnson.* Hattford, Conn.: Trinity College Press, 1928. An argument that Poe, unlike Coleridge, got his material from books rather than from nature.

BENTON, RICHARD P., ed. *New Approaches to Poe: a Symposium.* Hartford, Conn.: Transcendental Books, 1970. A collection of writings that indicate how and why Poe's reputation is on the rise.

———. *Poe as Literary Cosmologer. Studies on 'Eureka': a Symposium.* Hartford, Conn.: Transcendental Books, 1975. Analyses of possible meanings in Poe's prose-poem.

BLAIR, WALTER. "Poe's Conception of Incident and Tone in the Tale." *Modern Philology,* XLI (1944), 228-40. A good analysis of Poe's theory and practice in prose fiction.

BOLLE, JACQUES. *La Poésie du cauchemar.* Paris: Presse Française et Entrangère, 1946. A one-sided argument that Poe's psychological abnormalities are projected into his works.

BONAPARTE, MARIE. *The Life and Works of Edgar Allan Poe.* Translated by John Rodker. London: Imago, 1949. Psychoanalytical criticism at its worst.

BOND, FREDERICK DREW. "Poe as Evolutionist." *Popular Science Monthly,* LXXI (1907), 267-74. A serious treatment of "Eureka" as significant in the history of evolutionary thought from Thales to Darwin.

BOUSSOULAS, NICHOLAS-ISIDORE. *La Peur et l'univers dans l'oeuvre d'Edgar Poe: une métaphysique de la peur.* Paris: Presses Universitaires de France, 1952. Monograph that does not, and could not, prove its thesis that Poe's works are dominated by his fear of reality.

BRADDY, HALDEEN. *Glorious Incense: the Fulfillment of Edgar Allan Poe.* New York: Kennikat Press, 1963. Panorama of Poe's achievement and influence.

BROUSSARD, LOUIS. *The Measure of Poe.* Norman, Okla.: University of Oklahoma Press, 1969. A study that tries to find unity in Poe's works based on principles taken from "Eureka."

BROWNELL, W.C. *American Prose Masters: Cooper - Hawthorne - Emerson - Poe - Lowell - Henry James.* New York: Scribner's, 1909. A volume so derogatory of Poe that his appearance in it becomes an anomaly.

BURANELLI, VINCENT. "A Note on Poe and Mesmerism." *The Wizard from Vienna: Franz Anton Mesmer.* New York: Coward, McCann and Geoghegan, 1975. A chapter that places Poe against the background of the tradition founded by Mesmer.

CAMBIAIRE, CÉLESTIN P. *The Influence of Edgar Allan Poe in France.* New York: Stechert, 1927. Poe's literary legacy.

CAMPBELL, KILLIS. *The Mind of Poe and Other Studies.* Cambridge, Mass.: Harvard University Press, 1933. Important articles by one of the best commentators on Poe.

CANBY, HENRY SEIDEL. *Classic Americans.* New York: Harcourt Brace, 1931. The chapter on Poe regards him as a journalist who uses "tricks" to catch the attention and occasionally produces something worthwhile.

CARLSON, ERIC W., ed. *The Recognition of Edgar Allan Poe: Selected Criticism since 1829.* Ann Arbor, Mich.: University of Michigan Press, 1966. Judgments on Poe from his time to ours.

CHIARI, JOSEPH. *Symbolisme from Poe to Mallarmé.* London: Rockliff, 1956. A disparagement of Poe that questions that Mallarmé was as much indebted to Poe as he said he was.

CONNER, FREDERICK WILLIAM. "Poe's 'Eureka'; the Problem of Mechanism." *Cosmic Optimism: a Study of the Interpretation of Evolution by American Poets from Emerson to Robinson.* Gainesville, Fla.: University of Florida Press, 1949. Discussion of how Poe's work fits into this scientific tradition.

DAMERON, J. LASLEY. "Poe at Mid-Century: Anglo-American Criticism, 1928-1960." *Ball State University Forum,* VIII (1967), 36-44. A note on Poe's rising reputation in our time.

DAVIDSON, EDWARD H. *Poe: a Critical Study.* Cambridge, Mass.: Harvard University Press, 1957. An acutely reasoned, although sometimes far-fetched, interpretation of Poe and his place in the aesthetics of romanticism.

ELIOT, T.S. "From Poe to Valéry." *Hudson Review,* II (1949), 327-42. Analysis of Poe's literary legacy in France by a great poet with an ambiguous attitude toward Poe's poetry.

———. *Notes Towards the Definition of Culture.* New York: Harcourt Brace, 1949. One passage places Poe in a broader setting than the purely literary.

FAGIN, N. BRYLLION. *The Histronic Mr. Poe.* Baltimore: Johns Hopkins Press, 1949. Biography significant for revisionism in Poe scholarship because it pictures him as essentially an actor rather than as a case for the psychoanalysts.

FALK, DORIS V. "Poe and the Power of Animal Magnetism." *Publications of the Modern Language Association,* LXII (1969), 536-46. Explanation of Poe's literary use of Mesmer's cosmic theory.

FEIDELSON, CHARLES. *Symbolism and American Literature.* Chicago:

University of Chicago Press, 1953. Evaluation of Poe for his position in one broad current of our literary tradition.

FLETCHER, RICHARD M. *The Stylistic Development of Edgar Allan Poe.* The Hague: Mouton, 1973. A volume that, because of factual inaccuracies and implausible reasoning, does not live up to its title.

FOERSTER, NORMAN. *American Criticism: a Study in Literary Theory from Poe to the Present Day.* Boston: Houghton Mifflin, 1928. A treatise that forces the evidence to find contradictions in Poe.

FORCLAZ, ROGER. *Le Monde d'Edgar Poe.* Berne, Switzerland: Herbert Lang, 1974. A fine overall interpretation of Poe and his works.

FRIEDMAN, WILLIAM F. "Edgar Allan Poe, Cryptographer." *American Literature,* VII (1937), 266-80. An article that minimizes Poe's ability at solving ciphers.

GRIFFITH, CLARK. "Poe's 'Ligeia' and the English Romantics." *University of Toronto Quarterly,* XXIV (1954), 8-25. A dubious claim that this story is a satire on the Gothic horror tale.

GROSSMAN, JOAN DELANEY. *Edgar Allan Poe in Russia: a Study in Legend and Literary Influence.* Würzburg: Jal-Verlag, 1973. Description of how Poe affected such Russian masters as Dostoevski.

GRUBB, GERALD G. "The Personal and Literary Relationships of Dickens and Poe." *Nineteenth Century Fiction,* V (1950), 1-22, 101-20, 209-21. Poe's critical insight in recognizing the merits of Dickens.

GRUENER, GUSTAV. "Notes on the Influence of E.T.A. Hoffmann upon Edgar Allan Poe." *Publications of the Modern Language Association,* XIX (1904), 1-25. Description of Poe as strongly under Hoffmann's influence at the start, and then growing away from it.

HALLIBURTON, DAVID. *Edgar Allan Poe: a Phenomenonological View.* Princeton, N.J.: Princeton University Press, 1973. Relentlessly metaphysical readings that leave one wondering if Poe was not, after all, writing poems and tales without deep philosophical prepossessions.

HALLINE, ALLAN G. "Moral and Religious Concepts in Poe." *Bucknell University Studies,* II (1951), 126-50. Defense of Poe as more ethical and theological than is commonly thought.

HOAGLAND, CLAYTON. "The Universe of 'Eureka'." *Southern Literary Messenger,* new series, I (1939). Parallel study of Poe and Edington, the conclusion of which is that Poe had achieved something like the modern theory of the expanding universe.

HOFFMAN, DANIEL G. *Poe Poe Poe Poe Poe Poe Poe.* Garden City, N.Y.: Doubleday, 1972. Overly cute although occasionally perceptive interpretation of Poe's works through unity of images.

HOWARTH, WILLIAM L., ed. *Twentieth Century Interpretations of Poe's Tales: a Collection of Critical Essays.* Englewood Cliffs, N.J.: Prentice-Hall, 1971. Judgments on Poe's achievement in his major field.

HUBBELL, JAY B. *The South in American Literature.* Durham, N.C.: Duke University Press, 1954. A high appreciation of Poe as a sane creative artist.

HUNGERFORD, E. "Poe and Phrenology." *American Literature,* II (1930), 209-31. Proof that Poe regarded phrenology as a science.

HUXLEY, ALDOUS. "Vulgarity in Literature." In *Music at Night and Other Essays.* London: Chatto and Windus, 1930. An attempt to discredit Poe as a poet that actually discredits Huxley as a critic.

JACOBS, ROBERT D. *Poe, Journalist and Critic.* Baton Rouge, La.: Louisiana State University Press, 1969. The best book on Poe as a hard-working editor and reviewer.

JALOUX, EDMOND. *Edgar Poe et les femmes.* Geneva: Editions du Milieu du Monde, 1942. Realistic monograph on Poe's relations with women; useful corrective to psychoanalytical criticism.

JONES, HOWARD MUMFORD. "Poe, 'The Raven,' and the Anonymous Young Man." *Western Humanities Review,* IX (1955), 127-38. A persuasive defense of Poe against the "tawdry tinsel" school of criticism.

KELLY, GEORGE. "Poe's Theory of Beauty." *American Literature,* XXVII (1956), 521-36. Good analysis of Poe's notion of beauty and its ultimate derivation from Plato by way of Schlegel.

KESTERSON, DAVID B., ed. *Critics on Poe.* Coral Gables, Fla.: University of Miami Press, 1973. Anthology of excerpts from writers the editor considers significant.

KRUTCH, JOSEPH WOOD. *Edgar Allan Poe: a Study in Genius.* New York: Knopf, 1926. Elaborate and futile effort to prove that Poe was little more than a psychopathic case.

LAFLEUR, L. J. "Edgar Allan Poe as Philospher." *The Personalist,* XXII (1941), 401-5. Brief description of "Eureka," which is taken to be important in its approach to cosmology even though wrong in many details.

LASER, MARVIN. "The Growth and Structure of Poe's Concept of Beauty." *Journal of English Literary History,* XV (1948), 69-84. A reply to the charge that Poe's principles of aesthetics are incoherent.

LAUVRIÈRE, EMILE. *Le Génie morbide d'Edgar Poe.* Paris: Alcan, 1935. Discussion of the poems and stories that reads too much autobiography into their Gothic characters.

LAWRENCE, D.H. *Studies in Classical American Literature.* London: Seltzer, 1924. Essays by a great writer who mistakenly sees Poe as essentially reflected in his horror stories.

LEMONNIER, LÉON. *Edgar Poe et les conteurs francais.* Paris: Aubier, 1947. Handy sketch of the French prose writers influenced by Poe.

LENHART, CHARMENZ S. *Musical Influence on American Poetry.* Athens, Ga.: University of Georgia Press, 1956. The chapter on Poe argues that he had a good understanding of music as art and science, and of the application of music to poetry.

LEVIN, HARRY. *The Power of Blackness: Hawthorne, Poe, Melville.* New York: Knopf, 1958. A "literary iconology" that explains Poe's handling of horror and terror through an analysis of his imagery.

LEVINE, STUART. *Edgar Poe, Seer and Craftsman.* Deland, Fla.: Everett/Edwards, 1972. Interesting description of the two sides of Poe and their interaction, but too inclined to interpret him in terms of occult mysticism.

———. "Scholarly Strategy: The Poe Case." *American Quarterly,* XVII (1965), 133-44. An argument that criticism, like scholarship, should be cumulative. Some animadversions on my book led to the reply, "Judgment on Poe," ibid., 259-60.

LIND, S. E. "Poe and Mesmerism." *Publications of the Modern Language Association,* LXII (1947), 1077-94. Poe's interest in hypnotism and his handling of the motif in his writings.

LOCKSPEISER, EDWARD. *Debussy et Edgar Poe: Manuscrits et documents inédits.* Monaco: Editions du Rocher, 1961. Texts, commentaries, and notes that reveal the extraordinary influence of a great writer on a great composer.

———. "Debussy and Edgar Allan Poe." *The Listener* (1962), 609-10. A radio talk on the essentials of the above.

LUBELL, ALBERT J. "Poe and A.W. Schlegel." *Journal of English and Germanic Philology,* LII (1953), 1-12. An article that investigates Poe's debt to Schlegel, and claims that Poe is spoofing in his horror stories more than is generally realized.

MABBOTT, THOMAS O. *The Books in the House of Usher.* Reprint from *Books at Iowa,* XIX (1973). Poe had a good knowledge of bibliography when he drew up the list of Roderick Usher's favorite volumes.

——— "On Poe's 'Tales of the Folio Club'." *Sewanee Review,* XXXVI (1928), 171-76. A scholarly discussion of the book that Poe never published.

MCLUHAN, HERBERT MARSHALL. "Edgar Poe's Tradition." *Sewanee Review,* LII (1944), 24-33. Description of Poe as the only cosmopolitan man of letters in the nineteenth-century America, and as a product of the Ciceronian tradition of the South.

MARCHAND, ERNEST. "Poe as a Social Critic." *American Literature,* VI (1934), 28-43. Pictures Poe as very concerned with political and social problems from the standpoint of an intellectual and a Southern gentleman.

MARION, DENIS. "La Méthode intellectuelle de Poe." *Mesures,* VI (1940), 89-127. A critical investigation of Poe's use of analysis in logic.

MATTHIESSEN, FRANCIS O. "Poe." *Sewanee Review,* LIV (1946), 28-43. Laudatory essay on Poe's achievement.

MAUCLAIR, CAMILLE. *Le Genie d'Edgar Poe.* Paris: Michel, 1925. A good study of Poe from the point of view that his art is autonomous, almost entirely a product of his creative imagination, little related to his personal experiences.

MESSAC, RÉGIS. *Le 'Detective Novel' et l'influence de la pensée. scientifique.* Paris: Picard, 1929. A massive treatise that allots Poe a major share in the development of this literary genre.

MEYERSON, EMILE *Du Cheminement de la pensée.* Paris: Alcan, 1931. A highly sophisticated analysis of logic and the philosophy of science that mentions Poe as a preçurser because of "Eureka."

MILLER, JAMES, JR. " 'Ulalme' Resurrected." *Philological Quarterly,* XXXIV (1955), 197-205. Defense of Poe's poetry beginning with this famous example.

MILLER, PERRY. *The Raven and the Whale: the War of Words and Wits in the Era of Poe and Melville.* New York: Harcourt Brace, 1956. Humorous but scholarly account of the manner in which Poe became embroiled with New York's literati.

MOONEY, STEPHEN L. "The Comic in Poe's Fiction." *American Literature,* XXXIII (1962), 433-41. Vindication of Poe's comic talent on the basis of Bergson's theory of humor.

MOSS, SIDNEY P. *Poe's Literary Battles: the Critic in the Context of His Literary Milieu.* Durham, N.C.: Duke University Press, 1963. Persuasive treatment of Poe and his opponents; notable on Poe versus Longfellow.

———. *Poe's Major Crisis: His Libel Suit and New York's Literary World.* Durham, N.C.: Duke University Press, 1970. Valuable anthology of original views and comments.

NORSTEDT, GEORGE. "Poe and Einstein." *Open Court,* XLIV (1930), 173-80. The boldest attempt to prove that Poe anticipated central ideas of twentieth-century science.

Poe Studies, formerly *Poe Newsletter.* Pullman, Wash.: Washington State University Press, 1968-. The clearinghouse for everything that has to do with Poe.

POLLIN, BURTON R. *Discoveries in Poe.* Notre Dame, Ind.: Notre Dame University Press, 1970. Comprehensive investigations of Poe's sources.

PORGES, IRWIN. *Edgar Allan Poe.* Philadelphia: Chilton Books, 1963. Short biography that gives a balanced picture of the man and his works.

PRITCHARD, JOHN PAUL. *Criticism in America.* Norman, Okla.: University of Oklahoma Press, 1956. A history that judiciously isolates Poe as the first of the great American critics.

QUINN, ARTHUR HOBSON. *Edgar Allan Poe: a Critical Biography.* New York: Appleton-Century-Crofts, 1941. The best all-around book on Poe.

QUINN, PATRICK F. *The French Face of Edgar Poe.* Carbondale, Ill.: Southern Illinois Press, 1957. The best explanation of how and why Poe gained his enormous reputation in France.

———. *Poe and France: the Last Twenty Years.* Baltimore: Enoch Pratt Free Library, 1970. The subject brought up to date through a consideration of a new generation of French scholars and critics.

RANS, GEOFFREY. *Edgar Allan Poe.* Edinburgh: Oliver and Boyd, 1965. Good critical study; fair summing up of Poe as a poet and prose writer.

REGAN, ROBERT, ed. *Poe: a Collection of Critical Essays.* Englewood Cliffs, N.J.: Prentice-Hall, 1967. Opinions for and against Poe, the general tenor of which is favorable to him.

RICHARD, CLAUDE. "Poe Studies in Europe: France." *Poe Newsletter,* II (1969), 20-23. Review-article by a scholar who judiciously estimates the worth of various types of criticism currently popular.

ROBBINS, J. ALBERT. "The State of Poe Studies." *Poe Newsletter,* I (1968), 1-2. Brief survey and call to action.

ROURKE, CONSTANCE. *American Humor: a Study of the National Character.* New York: Doubleday, 1931. Vindication of Poe's right to a place in our comic tradition.

ROUTH, JAMES. "Notes on the Sources of Poe's Poetry: Coleridge, Keats, Shelley." *Modern Language Notes,* XXIX (1914), 72-75. Comparison of poetic lines to show some of Poe's derivations.

SAINTSBURY, GEORGE. *A History of Criticism and Taste in Europe.* Edinburgh and London: Blackwood, 1904. Exhaustive survey that mentions Poe favorably as a critic and finds an essential soundness in "The Rationale of Verse."

SMITH, C. ALPHONSO. *Edgar Allan Poe: How to Know Him.* Indianapolis: Bobbs-Merrill, 1921. Still a good introduction to Poe, this older work makes many points about his humor and his social interests that have been rediscovered in our time.

SMITH, H.E. "Poe's Extension of His Theory of the Tale." *Modern Philology,* XVI (1918), 195-203. A note of the manner in which Poe perfected his unity of effect.

STOVALL, FLOYD. *Edgar Allan Poe the Poet: Essays Old and New on the Man and His Work.* Charlottesville, Va.: University of Virginia Press, 1969. The best volume on the stubject, by one of the old masters of Poe studies.

TATE, ALLEN. "The Angelic Imagination: Poe and the Power of Words." *Kenyon Review,* XIV (1952), 455-75. Analytical article that fails in its attempt to find Poe's disintegration of personality in his tales.

———. "Our Cousin, Mr. Poe." *Partisan Review,* XVI (1949), 1207-9. The author admits an affinity with Poe, (despite a poor opinion of him,) because he anticipated contemporary American mood from alienation to despair.

TAYLOR, WALTER FULLER. "Israfel in Motley." *Sewanee Review,* XLII (1934), 330-40. Refutation of the old canard about Poe, the melancholy psychopath.

THOMPSON, G.R. *Poe's Fiction: Romantic Irony in the Gothic Tales.* Madison, Wis.: University of Wisconsin Press, 1973. A monograph valuable for pointing to the irony in Poe but excessive in finding it nearly everywhere.

VALÉRY, PAUL. *Variétes.* Paris: Gallimard, 1923. Contains an appreciation of Poe's cosmology, and a defense of his right to be called a harbinger of subsequent scientific ideas.

VELER, RICHARD P., ed. *Papers on Poe: Essays in Honor of John Ward Ostrom.* Springfield, Ohio: Chantry Music Press, 1972. A *festschrift* for a leading Poe scholar..

WAGENKNECHT, EDWARD. *Edgar Allan Poe: the Man behind the Legend.* New York: Oxford University Press, 1963. Balanced consideration of Poe, his works, his achievement, and his influence.

WALCUTT, CHARLES C. "The Logic of Poe." *College English,* II (1941), 438-44. An exaggerated argument that Poe's aesthetic is incoherent.

WALSH, JOHN. *Poe the Detective: the Curious Circumstances Behind "The Mystery of Marie Roget.* New Brunswick, N.J.: Rutgers University Press, 1968. Poe is shown making changes in his story as the facts in the Mary Rogers murder case proved him wrong about the solution.

WEISS, MIRIAM. "Poe's Catterina." *Mississippi Quarterly,* XIX (1965-66), 29-33. A cat is a cat, even in Poe.

WELLS, HENRY W. *The American Way of Poetry.* New York: Columbia University Press, 1943. Poe is pictured in this study as a great poet and a great innovator in poetry.

WERNER, W. L. "Poe's Theories and Practice in Poetic Technique." *American Literature,* II (1930), 157-65. Analysis of Poe's union of sound and sense in his poetry.

WHIPPLE, WILLIAM. "Poe's Political Satire." *University of Texas Studies in English,* XXXV (1956), 81-95. Interpretation of certain Poe stories as burlesques on Jackson and Van Buren.

WIENER, PHILIP P. "Poe's Logic and Metaphysics." *The Personalist,* XIV (1933), 268-74. A short but cogent defense of Poe's philosophical understanding.

WILSON, EDMUND. *The Shock of Recognition.* New York: Doubleday, 1943. Selections from the great critics of American literature, including eleven of Poe's reviews introduced by a fine appreciation of his achievement in this field; also comments on Poe by Lowell, Whitman, D.H. Lawrence, Mallarmé, and Bayard Taylor.

WILSON, JAMES S. "The Devil Was in It." *American Mercury,* XXIV (1931), 215-20. Poe as a satirist of the Gothic horror story.

WILT, NAPIER. "Poe's Attitude toward His Tales." *Modern Philology,* XXV (1927), 101-5. A warning that Poe is often trying for a shock reaction from his readers when he seems autobiographical.

WINTERS, YVOR. "Edgar Allan Poe: a Crisis in the History of American Obscurantism." *American Literature,* VIII (1937), 319-40. Reprinted in *Maule's Curse: Seven Studies in the History of American Obscurantism.* Norfolk, Conn.: New Directions, 1938. A thoroughgoing condemnation of Poe based on the quaint assumption that he is regarded as a great writer because Mr. Winters and "most of my friends" have been "sleeping."

WINWAR, FRANCES. *The Haunted Palace: a Life of Edgar Allan Poe.* New York: Harper, 1959. A biography that clings too closely to the metaphor in its title.

WOODBERRY, GEORGE E. *Edgar Allan Poe.* Boston: Houghton Mifflin, 1885. The earliest good critical biography of Poe, and still worth consulting.

WOODSON, THOMAS, ed. *Twentieth Century Interpretations of "The Fall of the House of Usher."* Englewood Cliffs, N.J.: Prentice-Hall, 1969. Critics discuss Poe's famous Gothic tale.

Index